Christmas in Devon

St Nectan's Church, Hartland

Christmas in Devon

Todd Gray

THE MINT PRESS

For Betsey

First published in Great Britain by The Mint Press, 2000

ISBN 1-903356-03-2

The Mint Press
18 The Mint
Exeter, Devon
England EX4 3BL

Typeset in Caslon 10.5/12.5 and Americana 10.5/12.5
by Quince Typesetting

Cover design by Delphine Jones

Printed and bound in Great Britain
by Short Run Press Ltd, Exeter.

Contents

Introduction

The celebration of Christmas in Devon has continually evolved over the centuries and there are few ways in which each generation's experiences have been similar. One exception involves the riddles found in Christmas crackers such as one in 1897: 'what is always behind time?' – 'the back of a watch'.[1] For the last hundred years it is clear that they have neither improved or indeed changed much. But the notion of a 'traditional Christmas' is a modern fixation and this book demonstrates that, as with all festivals, society has continually changed the way it marks the day and that there is no traditional Christmas: food, decorations, gifts and cards, music and entertainment, church attendance, and even the amount of time off from working have each changed with every subsequent generation. Moreover, Devon has celebrated Christmas in ways slightly different from the rest of the country. This book draws examples on how Christmas has been celebrated from the late thirteenth century up to the second world war, in most cases from first-hand accounts. Personal reminiscences, newspaper reports, jokes, recipes, cards, cartoons, poems, short stories and documents from the local archives are used to explain the celebration of Christmas in Devon. Very little has been written about the celebration of Christmas in Devon,[2] or in the rest of the country, and these examples have been selected to show the variety of different experiences in the county.

Many writers, particularly those writing memoirs, have insisted that society has changed for the worse in the way Christmas has been observed: the main complaint each generation makes is that the old customs are no longer being kept up. Autobiographers reminisce about their childhood and relate tales of happier days gone by. But it should be remembered that these memories involve a period in their lives when Christmas was provided for them rather than when as adults they were involved in providing Christmas for subsequent children. The holiday was, simply, a more innocent and carefree time, in effect, they experienced what is popularly called the 'magic' of Christmas.

This could be implied to mean that Christmas has always been celebrated – it was not. In the 1640s and 1650s tremendous efforts were made by Parliament to stop any celebrations. In those years, in what could be called a second Reformation, the celebration of Christmas was identified as a Catholic occasion as Easter became

Christmas cards sent to Devonians, both probably pre-Second World War

the more prominent date in the Protestant liturgical calendar. By the middle of the seventeenth century this was a longstanding concern particularly with much earlier moves to reduce attention to the Virgin Mary. Moreover, Christmas was derided as an immoral period of 'misrule' with excess drunkenness and promiscuity.[3] There is little evidence to show whether in Devon the national restrictions were obeyed although in 1642 a puritan minister from Mid-Devon gave a sermon at Exeter ridiculing the 'Lords of Misrule'.[4] However, in 1652, one visitor from London gleefully reported that Devon farmers maintained the old customs.[5]

Traditional cards – a hunting motif.

It could be argued that in the centuries before this stoppage there was at least a uniformity in the observance of Christmas. Through the medieval period under the Roman Catholic Church and then once again, for more than a century, from the creation of the Church of England in the early sixteenth century through to the Civil War of the 1640s, England was a one-religion state. Departure from attendance at the local church, to take part in other forms of worship, was punishable by heavy fines. In the 350 years or so since then society has had a fragmented observation of Christmas directly due to the increasing freedom to make personal choices in religion. Along with the gradual relaxation of religious law allowing the establishment of other Protestant churches, including Baptists, Methodists, Unitarians and Bible Christians, so has the observance of Christmas changed: each of these churches has different views on how to mark Christmas even if merely in the choice of music. Moreover, the gradual relaxation of laws allowing the return of the Roman Catholic Church into England and the importing of various American churches, including the Church of the Latter Day Saints, Christian Scientists and the Jehovah Witnesses, has further fragmented views on Christmas with the latter disregarding it as a day of celebration. Finally, as the country has become increasing multi-cultural, even if not so much so in Devon, but arguably already expressed for many centuries by the Jewish portion of the population, has made the marking of Christmas as a religious festival a nonsense for Buddhists, Hindus and Muslims amongst many others. Edmund Gosse was one such non-observer: in 1857 his father, a Plymouth Brethren, discovered that his servants had smuggled in a Christmas Pudding, which he considered an 'accursed thing', and ejected it from the kitchen onto the bonfire.[6] The differences with which Christians celebrate within their chosen churches is shown by the indignation of the editor of *The Western Times* in 1865 regarding the holding of Midnight Mass at Teignmouth. He wrote that the parishioners 'however tolerant and liberal-minded they may be in dealing with their fellow Christians of every shade of belief, it is more than human to expect they will suffer these bitter pills of popery to be thrust down their throats without an effort at resistance'. There was even less tolerance allowed the members of the Salvation Army in 1883 when they were set upon by a group of youths in Exeter. Likewise in Plymouth in 1847 one writer to the local newspaper commented upon how un-Christian it was, particularly at Christmas, for supposedly pious Protestants to express their prejudices against the poorly-fed and dressed Irish Catholics he watched going to Mass.[7]

One of the greatest obstacles for historians trying to understand Christmas is that the actual date for Christ's birthday is unknown. The New Testament does not provide one and the twenty-fifth day of December was formally determined as the date as late as the year 354. The legitimacy of it has always been questioned: some early writers placed the event as taking place during the spring. It was no accident that placing Christmas on 25 December coincided with an existing period of pagan worship: the Romans began to worship Saturn in mid-December and continued, with celebrations geared toward the new year, through to the first days of January. This was a chief day to revere the sun on the winter solstice and the beginning of a new year, conveniently for the early Christian church it was the time of rebirth. The early Christian Church absorbed these pagan days by extending the Christmas season to include the baptism of Jesus by John the Baptist and the Adoration of the Magi on 6 January. The observance of Christmas in the medieval period continued to be caught up with celebrating midwinter with the addition of the Scandinavian pagan term 'Yule' being adopted by the English. As late as the end of the twelfth century Batholomew Iscanus, bishop of Exeter, was concerned that his parishioners observed the new year with pagan ceremonies.[8]

Little is known of how Christmas was spent in the Medieval period but certainly the observance of it as a religious festival was accompanied by marking it as a holiday period. In effect, for many people, Christmas has remained a time of relaxation and enjoyment, most likely a residue of the older pagan customs. A hint of Christmas customs in the pre-Reformation years was given in comments by Archbishop Thomas Cranmer in 1549 on the Westcountry Prayer Book Rebels:

But where you say that you will have the old service, because the new is 'like a Christmas game', you declare yourselves what spirit you be led withal, rather what spirit leadeth them that persuade you that the word of God is but like a Christmas game. It is more like a game and a fond play to be laughed at of all men, to hear the priest speak aloud to the people in Latin, and the people listen with their ears to hear and some walking up and down in the church, some saying other prayers in Latin, and none understanding [each] other. Neither the priests nor his parish wot [know] what they say. And many times the thing that the priest sayeth in Latin is so fond of itself, that it is more like a play than a godly prayer.[9]

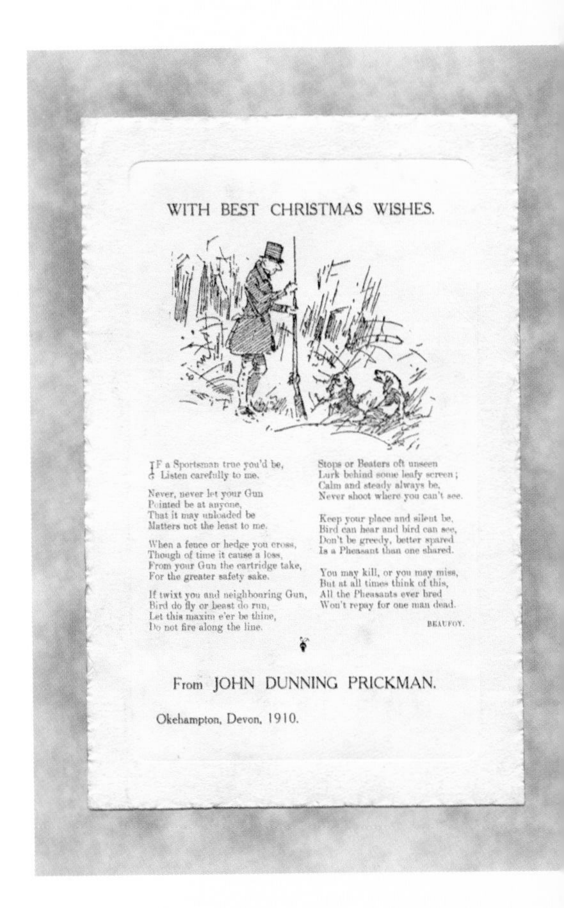

The Christmas game he refers to appears to have been a light-hearted occasion, possibly a play or least a public performance of some kind. Similar events are known to have been held in parish churches, generally the largest building in a parish, throughout the county including Ashburton, Barnstaple, Plymouth and Plymstock.[10] Because of the time of year they had to be indoor events. Other celebrations were held in the houses of the gentry or in large farmhouses. These took the form of a large meal provided either for tenants of the manor or for workers and their families. In about 1610 John Willoughby, then resident at Combe in Gittisham, provided a series of meals over six days in the season for his tenants and workers.[11] It was probably for such an occasion that in 1718 Sir William Pole, resident at Shute in East Devon, had a bull slaughtered four days before Christmas[12] and that in 1816 the kitchen at Castle Hill near South Molton was provided with

Some of the cards received by Earl Fortescue, Lord Lieutenant of Devon, during the First World War.

nearly 700 pounds of beef, 113 pounds of mutton and 77 pounds of veal by the Fortescue family.[13]

However well-intentioned, this providing of largesse by the gentry was not fondly remembered by everyone. In 1876 a resident of Kingsbridge wrote that in the years before the Great Reforms of the 1830s the ordinary Devon villager was reliant upon the wealthy to provide a Christmas meal for which he would 'render obedience to his betters until Christmas came round again'. In the following years, he wrote, the standard of living had risen to allow workers to provide a meal for themselves in their own homes. Moreover, it was felt that the practices of asking for charity either by "a'gooding", in which women dressed in their poorest clothes on Christmas Eve and knocked on the doors of the wealthy, and by 'mumping', in which women, children and infirm men walked through the streets begging for money or goods, were both highly demeaning. He strongly felt that the 'good old times' never were.[14] Interestingly, in 1831 a Devon commentator urged the local wealthy, in a newspaper article entitled 'Old English Hospitality', to provide the poor with food because otherwise the county would suffer the arson attacks then prevalent in the rest of the country. It would, he wrote, 'conciliate the oppressed poor'.[15]

Historians have questioned whether wealthy householders began to decrease their largesse as early as the seventeenth century but certainly by the early nineteenth century, with the rise of larger urban populations, the large meal of the manorial lord was less socially prominent and large landed estates increasingly provided gifts of meat or items of clothing. On a parish level, money and items of clothing were often given to the poor: for example, a Silverton man gave funds in 1613 to provide wool clothing for poorer people in his parish.[16] In towns Christmas boxes were given to various workers. In 1865 'Tiny Tim' wrote to *The Exeter Flying Post* pleading for this seasonal money to be continued to be given to postmen and errand boys but a year later 25 of the city's tea dealers and grocers placed an advertisement to give public notice they has stopped the practice.[17] Inmates in gaols and workhouses were generally given a large Christmas meal, the men provided with tobacco and the women and children with oranges and sweets.

Victorian charity largely centred on the deserving poor, children and the infirm. In 1874 the editor of *The Devon Weekly Times* cautioned his readers against wishing for a white Christmas. He wrote in contrast to some enthusing about seasonal frosty days, the 'ill-fed, the thinly-clad and badly-housed' the colder weather merely caused further suffering.[18] One of the most well-known events was put on annually by Harry Hems, the Exeter craftsman. On Christmas Day in 1889, for the twenty-first consecutive year, he provided a feast of beef, mutton, pork and goose for some 60 'broken-down citizens and their wives' in his studio on Longbrook Street and again on Boxing Day he and his family entertained the children from a local orphanage. At Tavistock in 1888 220 wives and children of the Navvies were given a Christmas tea together with gifts and an entertainment. The children at the Starcross Asylum had an annual Christmas treat; in 1891 they sang carols, ate plum cake and oranges, pulled crackers and were told that the sum of three pounds was to be spent on toys for them. In the late nineteenth century the poor children of Exeter were known as 'the Robins' and given an annual Christmas meal. A newspaper report provides the atmosphere for the event held in 1893: whether it was due to the exhilarating effect of the currant buns and tea or the exuberance which should be natural to the rising generation matters not, but at one interval a cherub of a youngster, pouting up his pretty mouth, whispered as loud as his extended cheeks would allow the magical words of *Dai-sy, Dai-sy*. It spread like scarlet fever in a boarding school and in half a minute from nine hundred straining throats went up a deafening *Give me your answer true*.[19]

Not all celebrations have been so cherubic. A continual aspect to the social side to Christmas has been complaints of the excessive enthusiasm with which some celebrate: drunkenness has been associated with Christmas for hundreds of years. In 1725 Andrew Brice sympathised with the citizens of Exeter on Christmas Eve: 'Woe to you peaceful inhabitants, whose lodging apartments front the troubled streets!' Just over a hundred years later it was the gin shop at Christmas which attracted interest. One wag wrote:

> A gin shop is a wicked place
> A place of low degree
> Tis where the tipplers go to learn
> Their Gin-eology.

The writer wrote further lines on the dangers of gin.[20] Late nineteenth-century newspapers are full of reports of drunkenness over Christmas: for example, in Exeter in 1883 Charles Johns, a cattle drover, was charged with being drunk and causing a nuisance: it was reported that at one o'clock on Christmas morning he had been 'hooting and shouting' and annoying a party singing carols before a house in Belmont Road.[21] There were also abstemious Christmases: in 1846 it was reported from Plymouth that the congregation of the Plymouth Temperance Society were 'very healthy-looking … and their countenances would furnish a good character for the excellence of their principles'.[22]

The consumption of food features in nearly every account of Christmas. Roast beef seems to have been the more popular choice for a main meal until the middle of the nineteenth century when turkey appears to take over. Goose was the other favoured meat. Plum pudding was an early favourite although those made from figs are occasionally mentioned. One great feature of nineteenth-century Christmas was the annual Meat Show put on by butchers: in mid-December shoppers would admire the displays of great mounds of meat which represented not just holiday feasting but the general productivity of the land.

Sport of various kinds has been a feature of Boxing Day for many generations. Many Victorian Christmas cards featured a hunting scene because of the meeting of hunts on the 26th of December. A report of a match in 1891 shows the importance of other sporting events:

The chief attraction of the holidays was the visit of the Barbarians to Exeter, and in spite of frost, fog, rain and the absence of excursion trains from South

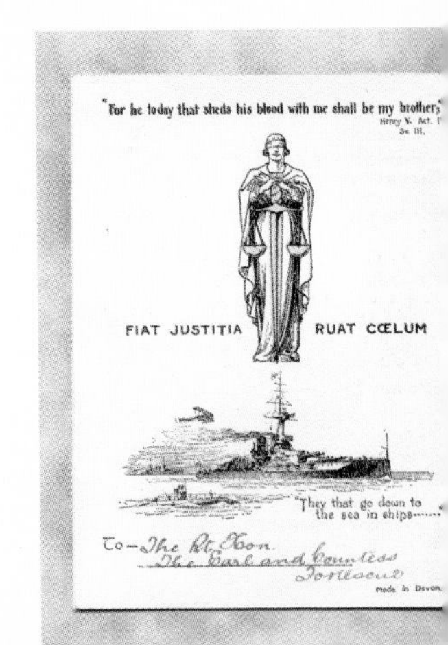

A New Zealand card sent to Devon.

Devon and elsewhere, the fixture should stand among the best of recent years. Either Devon is improving or the Barbs had had rather too much Christmastide, but whichever it was the crowd which lined the enclosure at St Thomas on Saturday was mightily pleased with the performance of the home players. A friend who travelled sixty miles to witness the encounter says he considers it worth all the money he spent in going to and from the ground, and I think those players who took my advice and put in an appearance will agree that they were able to learn a few useful lessons form some of the best exponents of the game in the country.[23]

The terminology of Christmas has also evolved. Seasonal wishes for a 'Merry Christmas' appear to have been more common in the nineteenth century after which 'Happy Christmas' comes into more common usage. The use of 'Xmas' for Christmas is more longstanding than is perhaps widely known: local newspapers often preferred Xmas in the late nineteenth century and even the earliest parish registers, as far back as the mid sixteenth century, abbreviated the name Christopher to 'Xpher'. But the practice is much older than that: X is the abbreviated form of Christ because it is the first letter of Greek Χριστος (khristos). Perhaps the best example of changing terminology and custom is in the use of the figure used to represent the spirit of Christmas. Father Christmas, Santa Claus and St Nicholas were all used in the nineteenth century; for instance in 1897 one Exeter man, Harry Hems, was reported to have 'acted the part of Santa Claus'.[24] This figure, personifying Christmas, merged with St Nicholas, the medieval patron of children. In the first part of the nineteenth century the figure of St Nicholas was reintroduced to American readers with Clement Clark Moore's 'A Visit from St Nicholas'. His saint was a magical character with a white beard who travelled through the air on a reindeer-drawn sleigh. Within a generation the story was incorporated within English culture. Through the nineteenth century his clothing changed to the colour red.[25]

The music of Christmas is another long-standing feature. Carollers, and earlier the waits, serenaded the streets of many villages and towns particularly very early on Christmas morning. With the proliferation of churches there arose rivalry between the choirs. For example, in 1897 at Hartland it was reported:

It is certainly at any time a pity for two choirs to sing with all the power of their lungs, different tunes at the same time and place, but especially in commemoration of the visit to this earth of the angel choir on the first Christmas morning; such inharmonious rivalry is out of place. Babel being neither conducive to 'Glory to God in the Highest' nor to 'Peace on earth, good-will to all men'.[26]

The Reverend Baring-Gould remembered that in 1862 the parish singers refrained from visiting the parson because he did not tolerate the music of dissenting churches. There was bad singing reported at Bideford in 1866 and but at Exmouth ten years later there were further complaints about the effect of rival choirs singing in close proximity. A German brass band was disapproved of at Sidmouth in 1865 but the stronger objection was made at Dartmouth in 1876 after a group of drunken sailors serenaded the town with vulgar songs and blue jokes.

There have been particular Christmas customs within Devon which have spanned several generations. Some sayings had local usage such as 'A Green Christmas makes a fat churchyard[27] and there are superstitions such as in West Devon where allegedly it was believed that on Christmas Eve oxen kneeled in memory of the birth of Christ.[28] However, in respect to decorations, fire-burning, wassailing and mummers there appears to have been customs which went on for several generations. If Robert Herrick was right, then holly and other greenery has been used in Devon for many hundreds of years. The poet, largely based at Dean Prior, noted rosemary, bay, mistletoe, holly and ivy as decorative plants. In 1882 at Exeter there was a report that 'The steamer Ossian came up to the quay on Christmas Eve laden with brandy. On Christmas Day she had boughs of mistletoe suspended from the mastheads and her bowspirit'.[29] The use of mistletoe may not have been widespread as Herrick suggests. At Bideford a kissing ring, some five to six feet in diameter and constructed of holly and other evergreens, was common in the late nineteenth century. Nearby at Hartland at the same time it was more usual in at least one household to hang from the centre of the ceiling a kissing bush which was not formed of mistletoe 'for that was unknown to us – 'the mistletoe doesn't grow where the nightingale doesn't sing' – but consisting of a small bush of vuz (furse), which was damped, sprinkled with flour and studded with holly berries'.[30] By the middle of the nineteenth century the German practice of bringing trees into the house was becoming popular. Initially, it appears as though light-weight presents were placed on the branches of the tree, often in situations where public charity was being distributed such as at orphanages or hospitals. Decorations could be very innovative. In the late nineteenth century Japanese lanterns were popular and paper decorations were also greatly used. At Devonport in 1879 the men of the Army Service Corps used 2,000 pieces of coloured paper for a centre piece representing the Wheel of Life but there were also illuminated models and a water colour sketch of a team and wagon. In 1911 bunches of holly were attached to the mastheads of the warships at Devonport while in Torquay the hospital had red, white and blue decorations in the Coronation Ward, a representation of 'the lady of the lamp' in the Florence Nightingale Ward and the Children's Ward was decorated to resemble the seaside with sand, boats and bathing tents.

In Devon the Yule Log took the shape of the 'Ashen Faggot'. These bundles of thick ash were bound with withies and as each binding burst a round of drinks was enjoyed by the company. Wassailing was another custom practiced in the West Country. At Christmas, and in the days that followed, a variety of songs were sung in orchards order to encourage a good crop of apples for the forthcoming season. There were many variations of the verse. In the early seventeenth century Robert Herrick, vicar of Dean Prior, penned verses to wassailing:

> Wassail the trees, that they may bear
> You many a plum and many a pear;
> For more or less fruits they will bring,
> As you do give them wassailing.[31]

In the South Hams another variation in 1791 ran:

> Here's to thee, old apple tree,
> Whence thou mayst bud
> And whence thou mayst blow!
> And whence thou mayst bear apples enow!
> Hats full! Caps full!
> Bushel – bushel – sacks full,
> And my pockets full too! Huzza![32]

Early on in the next century another verse from the South Hams was sung:

> Huzza, Huzza, in our good town
> The bread shall be white, and the liquor be brown
> So here my old fellow I drink to thee
> And the very health of each other tree.
> Well may ye blow, well may ye bear
> Blossom and fruit both apple and pear.
> So that every bough and every twig
> May bend with a burden both fair and big
> May ye bear us and yield us fruit such a stores
> That the bags and chambers and house run o'er.[33]

The final custom which appears to have been common in Devon in the eighteenth and nineteenth centuries, and probably before as well, were the Mummers who performed to the public in larger houses. For example, on the second of January in 1740 one shilling was given at a gentry house in South Devon to Father Christmas. He was, presumably, a Mummer.[34] The earliest known manuscript description of a mummer play is by Andrew Brice of Exeter in 1738. The descriptions of their clothing differ, much of it seems to have been fancy or exotic clothes, but many accounts show there was Father Christmas, a hero, generally St George, and a villain, originally a Turkish knight. In the early nineteenth century the hero was replaced either by the Duke of Wellington or Lord Nelson and the villain by Napoleon. All mummers appear to have been disguised in some manner, whether by masks or in the blackening of faces. In the nineteenth century they were part of a form of entertainment which regularly used black faces and merged with the minstrels. For example, a troupe of 'Amateur Darkies' played at Topsham in 1892 and at Budleigh Salterton on Christmas Eve in 1874 the entertainment included 'Niggers, too, with blackened faces and frizzy polls were singing in Negro patois their war songs, and otherwise imitating them by dancing in the moonlight'. This was repeated on Boxing Day for the 'the whole place ran revel, every one did what he considered right in his own eyes, with mummers, niggers, singers, dancers, &c, a repetition of Christmas Eve performances'.[35]

Christmas was also a time to report unusual or odd events. One such tale was reported in 1875 at Dawlish under the heading 'Stranger on Boxing Day'.

A fine hare about noon, on Monday, was seen to run down by the Post Office, then through Beach Street, doubling near Piermont Place, and then doubled and from thence through the bar parlour of The Royal Albert Hotel, where puss was captured by Mr Carroll, the landlord, and by Bombardier Cole, Teignmouth Company Royal Artillery.[36]

Likewise in 1903 more than 100 men and women gathered on the Hoe at Plymouth for a Christmas morning dip and in 1887 it was reported that a collie dog wandered into the bell tower at Upottery Church while the bells were ringing and had his head entangled in the wheel but was, surprisingly, unhurt. Another odd report appeared *The Devon Weekly Times* in 1873 of Witheridge:

A large snake about three feet in length, having left its winter quarters on Monday, December 23rd, perhaps with the intention of spending a merry Christmas with some friends, was driven over by the coachman of E. Dyer, Esquire, in the coach road leading to Bradford Cottage.[37]

Perhaps one of the more peculiar incidents occurred in North Devon in 1883. Two days after Christmas the effigy of an unidentified person was paraded to the sound of singing and hand bells through the town of Ilfracombe and burnt on the Strand.

Feelings of good will, at Christmas and New Year, form part of the long celebrations from 25th of December through to Twelfth Night. Sentimentality was also a strong feature of the late Victorian short stories which were published during Christmas week: dream sequences, lost love and the rewarding of virtue all figure in the three stories reprinted in this book. Finally, one account is included entitled 'People Who Don't Celebrate Christmas'. A nineteenth century writer pointed out that many people were not able to celebrate, notably those involved in public service such as the police but there were others who resented having days off without work because it impoverished them unlike the majority of workers who enjoy paid holidays. Christmas has also been a time for expressing good wishes. Initially hand-made cards were sent in the nineteenth century. Few of the early mass-produced cards have survived. One notable series is a collection of cards sent to the Lord Lieutenant of the county during the first world war, many of which appear in the margins.

In the late nineteenth century one Devonian, the aptly named Mr Toogood, composed his own 'Christmas Greeting':

A Merry Christmas to all who are dear
And may happiness come with [a] bright new year
Old Loves be renewed, old friends brought more near
All faces be smiling and none shed a tear.[38]

A card written by a patient at the temporary hospital in Heavitree during the First World War.

A hand-made Devon card.

More First World War cards.

Notes

[1] See below, page 99.

[2] One of the few published works is Chris Smith, *A West Country Christmas* (Gloucester, 1989).

[3] Chris Durston, 'Lords of Misrule, the Puritan War on Christmas, 1642–60', *History Today*, December, 1985, 7–14.

[4] John M. Wasson, *Records of Early English Drama: Devon* (Toronto, 1986), 205; Mark Stoyle, *Loyalty and Locality* (Exeter, 1994), 226.

[5] See below, page 12.

[6] See below, page 51.

[7] See below, page 53, 75, 43.

[8] Ronald Hutton, *The Stations of the Sun* (Oxford, 1996), 1–8.

[9] John Edmond Cox (ed.), *Miscellaneous Writings and Letters of Thomas Cranmer* (Cambridge, 1846), I, 180.

[10] Wasson, *Records of Early English Drama: Devon*, 22–6, 34, 23, 237, 277.

[11] See below, page 9.

[12] Devon Record Office 235M/E5; 235M/E4. Two years earlier he had a pig and two bullocks killed.

[13] See below, page 27.

[14] See below, pages 34.

[15] See below, pages 36.

[16] Memorial erected on south external wall, Silverton Parish Church.

[17] See below, page 57.

[18] See below, pages 62.

[19] *The Devon Weekly Times*, 20 December 1893.

[20] See below, pages 15, 38.

[21] *The Western Times*, January 1884.

[22] See below, pages 42.

[23] *The Western Times*, 29 December 1891.

[24] *Exeter Flying Post*, 24 December 1897.

[25] Hutton, *Stations*, 117–119.

[26] *The Hartland Chronicle*, January 1898.

[27] R.P.C. Chope, *Dialect of Hartland* (1891), 17.

[28] Mrs Henry Pennell Whitcombe, *Bygone Days in Devonshire and Cornwall* (1874), 7.

[29] *The Western Times*, January 1883.

[30] See below, pages 61.

[31] Herrick, poem 787 quoted by R. Pearse Chope, 'Devonshire Calendar Customs: Part II', *Devonshire Association Transactions* (LXX, 1939), 353.

[32] *The Gentleman's Magazine*, 1791.

[33] British Library, Add. Mss 41313, fo.85 quoted by R. Hutton, *The Stations of the Sun* (Oxford, 1996), 46.

[34] Devon Record Office, 316M/EA13. I am grateful to Clare Greener for this reference.

[35] See below, pages 18, 31, 62.

[36] *The Western Times*, 31 December 1875.

[37] *The Devon Weekly Times*, 3 January 1873.

[38] Devon Record Office, 1788Z/Z1.

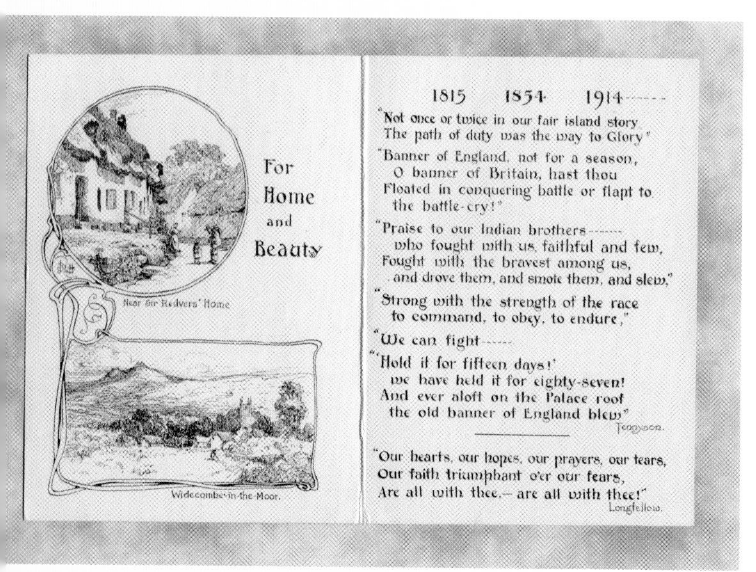

Acknowledgements

I would like to thank Margery Rowe, Margaret Westcott and Mary Reeves for their help with this book.

The Nativity in Devon's Churches and Exeter Cathedral

Exeter Cathedral

Exeter Cathedral

St Nectan's Church, Hartland

St Mary's Church, Totnes

St Mary's Church, Burlescombe

St Michael's Chapel of Ease, Exeter

St Mary Magdalene's Church, South Molton

St David's Church, Exeter

1285 Medieval Exeter's Royal Christmas: the visit of King Edward I and Queen Eleanor

On 22 December 1285 King Edward I and Queen Eleanor arrived in Exeter for a visit which extended over the Christmas period. They were accompanied by the Princesses Eleanor, Joan and Margaret and were the first Royal Family to spend Christmas in Exeter. Historians have disagreed on whether they stayed at Rougemont Castle, the Bishop's Palace or at the convent of the Black Friars (later Bedford House) but it is known that on their second day in the city, the 23rd of December, the family attended mass at the Cathedral. It was their first and only visit to Exeter but they were not in the city to enjoy the holidays: the king had travelled to Exeter at the request of the Bishop in order to investigate a case of murder.

More than two years previously, just after midnight, in the early hours of 9 November 1283, Walter Lechlade, the Precentor of the Cathedral, left Matins dressed in his full canonicals and accompanied by several of his servants and a lantern bearer. A few minutes before a certain Thomas, later revealed to be in the employ of the mayor, led several horses through South Street and into Cathedral Close. He sounded a small horn to alert his fellow conspirators and upon sighting Lechdale they attacked him with knives, swords and axes. Not only did they break his arm but struck two particularly severe blows to the head from which wounds he immediately died. The Precentor's servants had initially fled the attackers but the noise woke other nearby inhabitants and the murderers fled. Lechlade had been at the centre of a power struggle within the city. His main supporter was the Bishop but he was opposed by two other powerful men, namely the Dean, John Pycot, and the Mayor, Alfred de Porta. Lechlade's subsequent violent death implicated them both and subsequently the Mayor and four other men, but not the clerics, were arrested and brought to trial.

Justice appears to have moved quickly once the King opened proceedings. The trial began on Monday the 24th of December, adjourned on Christmas Day and resumed on Boxing Day. Shortly afterwards the mayor and the other four men were hanged for their complicity in the murder. The actual killers were thought to have escaped on the night of the murder through the South Gate which had been left unguarded; the Keeper of the Gate was one of the men executed. But the Dean and several other clergymen, including the vicars of Ottery St Mary and Heavitree, pleaded benefit of clergy and escaped execution. The Dean's punishment was banishment to a monastery. It was shortly after this incident that the Cathedral churchyard was enclosed by a high wall with several strong gates; thus creating Cathedral Close. The King and his Queen

1316
In Christmas Week a quarry labourer was paid eight pence for his work on Exeter Cathedral.

1318
Two carters working on Exeter Cathedral were paid two shillings for their wages in Christmas Week.

continued their stay in the city long enough to hold a session of Parliament before returning to London.[1]

Most likely the murder case dominated their Christmas festivities but there must have been some light-hearted entertainment as well. The proceedings made Christmas probably the most well remembered event that Exeter had seen for generations.

1337 Bishop Grandisson's Service for Christmas Eve at Exeter Cathedral

Sometime in about the year 1337 Bishop John Grandisson designed a service to celebrate Christmas Eve. In 1928, nearly six hundred years later, it was revived in Exeter Cathedral and set to music by the organist.[2] It has become Exeter's most popular service of the year. Grandisson gave long instructions with part of the order of the service being:

The first lesson being ended, and the reader thereof having returned to his stall, a boy-chorister, habited in a girded alb and an amice, and bearing in his left hand a light, takes his stand before the High Altar. Facing the Quire he sings:

Today for us the King of Heaven hath deigned to be born of a virgin.

To this announcement the choir responds:

That He might restore lost mankind. The angelic Host rejoiceth for that eternal salvation hath appeared to the children of men.

In the meantime the boy singer, proceeding westwards, is joined, first by six of his fellows, and then by two of the Priests-Vicars Choral habited in copes. Then the choir sings:

Glory to God in the highest; peace on earth to men of good will. Alleluia.

The Procession having come to the screen, the Priests hand on the glad tidings to the people assembled in the nave, repeating Hodie Nobis, etc., to which the seven boys respond:

Today the Lord hath shone upon us. Alleluia.

The choir then sings:

He cometh down from heaven and is made man. Glory to God, etc., Alleluia.

The Procession having returned to the Quire, the Office, ends with the *Magnificat*, with which Evensong continues.[3]

1522 A Plantagenet princess and Tiverton: Katherine, the 'Daughter, Sister and Aunt of Kings'

One of the few members of the Royal Family to ever live in Devon was a Plantagenet princess: Katherine, the daughter of Edward IV, and sister to the two missing 'Princes in the Tower', was born in 1479. In 1495 she married Sir William Courtenay but he died in 1512 leaving her a widow at the age of 33. She never remarried and died at Tiverton in 1527 at the age of 48. She styled herself 'Princess Katherine, Countess of Devon, daughter, sister and aunt of Kings' by virtue of being the daughter of Edward IV, sister of Edward V, sister-in-law of Henry VII and aunt to Henry VIII. She appears to have spent most of her widowhood in Devon, far from the intrigues and dangers of the Court, where her houses and estates included Okehampton Castle, Plympton Castle, Colcombe in Colyton, Columbjohn in Broadclyst and Tiverton Castle.

It would not be surprising that her Christmas was extravagant given her status as a Royal Princess but unfortunately only for one particular Christmas, that of 1523, have the records survived. Among the presents she gave to her son Henry were two buckles,

1319
Ten pence were spent on mats for Exeter's Chapter House in the week before Christmas.

1325
Two shillings and two pence were paid in Christmas Week to repair Walter, one of the Cathedral's bells.

1431
A Christmas play was performed in Exeter's Guildhall.

1476
A Christmas play was performed at Barnstaple.

1535
Players from Exeter performed a Christmas play in Ashburton church.

two pendants, six studs, six oiletts, six aglets, and gold and enamel garters. She also gave twenty shillings as general alms for the poor. The festivities extended from Christmas through to Twelfth Night and although the records are largely indecipherable there are some details of the provisions Princess Katherine purchased for Tiverton Castle. In addition to the four swans cooked on Christmas Day there was a gallon of honey, apples and warden pears. But she received a number of gifts which would have supplemented the provisions for any kitchen: she had a boar and two swans from Forde Abbey, two oxen from the bishop, and a boar and ox from two members of the gentry. She also bought two dozen supper lights, which weighed five pounds, and cost her three shillings and nine pence. The entertainment appears lavish: there were players on New Year's Eve and New Year's Day and the Waits of Exeter performed on Twelfth Night. The festivities appear to have been lavish as befitting a royal princess, the daughter, sister and aunt of kings.[4]

c.1610 A gentry Christmas at Gittisham

For several years in the early seventeenth century John Willoughby, Lord of the Manors of Farway, Gittisham and Feniton, lodged, with his family, in Gittisham at Combe, the home of Mrs Elizabeth Beaumont, a widow who may have been his godmother and known to her friends as Besee and even, BB. His own home, Leyhill in Payhembury, was occupied by his mother. Sometime in about 1610 Willoughby entertained 84 local villagers to a series of meals from Christmas to Twelfth Night. It was most likely an annual event. The document which lists the guests is unusual: no other comparative evidence survives for its period for the whole of Devon.[5] Other papers from his family papers illustrate the range of food he provided for ceremonial occasions. Willoughby's guests would have enjoyed a mixture of sweet and savoury food at the same sitting including pasties and pies (made from apples, pears, quinces as well as chicken, various wild birds, beef, marrow bones, salmon and pigeons), cuts of beef, mutton and pork, even including trotters, udders and calves' tongues, which may have been roasted or boiled, various types of fish both salt and fresh-water, and a wide range of vegetables including carrots, leeks, cabbages and parsnips. Cider, ale, beer and wines from France, Spain, Portugal and the Canary Islands were all popular beverages. The food was flavoured with such spices as ginger, nutmeg, cinnamon, saffron and pepper.

Christmas Day
12 guests
William Water & his wife
John Salter & his wife
Drewe & his wife
Baker & his wife
Alice & her daughter
Widow Bourne
John Water

St Steven's day (26 December)
13 guests
William German & his wife
Steven Goolde & his wife
Robert Burnerd & his wife
Walter Sannders & his wife
John Awton & his wife
Chanseller & his wife
Jane Salter & his wife

St John's Day (27 December)
13 guests
Richard Littlejohn & his wife
Philip Satterley & his wife
Richard Gover & his wife
John Genkin & his wife
Nicholas Morris & his wife
Edward Pease & his wife
Christopher Ellis

Innocent's Day (28 December)
13 guests
Thomas Littlejohn & his wife
John Baily & his wife
Richard Drewe & his wife
Joan Weelche & Alice Sannders
Walter Brooke & Martin Brooke
Robert Pratte & his wife
Michael Warren

for Sunday
21 guests
Joseph Vinicombe & his wife
Widow Vinicombe & W. Venne
Widow Powell & W: Drewe
Henry Monsteeven & his wife
Widow Salter
Holmes & his wife
Gover & his wife
Haydon & his wife
Christopher White & his wife
Lawrence White: Christopher Mathew
Henry Venn: Christopher Baily

Twelfth Day (6 January)
12 guests
Richard Potter & his wife
Widow Flea & her father
Amias Ellis & his wife
George Mitchell & his wife
Martin Sannder & Richard Marker
William Marker & his wife

1566
Totnes players performed a Christmas play at Plymouth.

1570
A Christmas play was performed in Plymstock church.

1590
On Boxing Day the Prudence *of Barnstaple arrived at Appledore with a Portuguese ship carrying a cargo including 4 chests of gold, captured on the African coast.*

1592
On Christmas Eve, Gonzalo Gonzales del Castillo, a prisoner since the defeat of the Armada four years before, sailed from Exeter for Britanny.

1596
There was continual rain in Barnstaple in the weeks running up to Christmas.

1630s Robert Herrick and Christmas at Dean Prior

Robert Herrick was rector of Dean Prior from 1629 to 1647 and again from 1662 to 1674. The poet is widely remembered to have preferred life in London to that he had in remote South Devon. Herrick wrote several poems on Christmas celebrations. One of them was on the Christmas Log.

Burning the Christmas Log

Come, bring with a noise,
My merry, merry boys,
The Christmas log to the firing;
While my good dame, she
Bids ye all be free,
And drink to your hearts' desiring.

With the last year's brand
Light the new block, and
For good success in his spending
On your psaltries play,
That sweet luck may
Come while the log is a-teending.

Drink now the strong beer,
Cut the white loaf here;
The while the meat is a-shredding
For the rare mince-pie,
And the plums stand by
To fill the paste that's a-kneading.

He also wrote poems on the long holiday celebrations of 7th of January and on Candlemas, the second of February.

St Distaff's Day or the Morrow after Twelfth Night

Partly work and partly play
You must on St Distaff's day
From the plough soon free your team,
Then come home and fodder them.
If the maids a-spinning go,
Burn the flax and fire the tow;
Scorch the pockets, but beware
That you singe no maiden-hair,
Bring in pails of water, then,
Let the maids bewash the men.
Give Saint Distaff all the right,
Then bid Christmas sport good-night;
And next morrow, every one
To his own vocation.

Candlemas Eve

Down with the rosemary, and so
  Down with the bays and mistletoe;
Down with the holly, ivy, all,
  Wherewith ye dressed the Christmas Hall:
That so the superstitious find
  No one least branch there left behind:
For look, how many leaves there be
  Neglected, there (maids trust to me)
So many goblins you shall see.

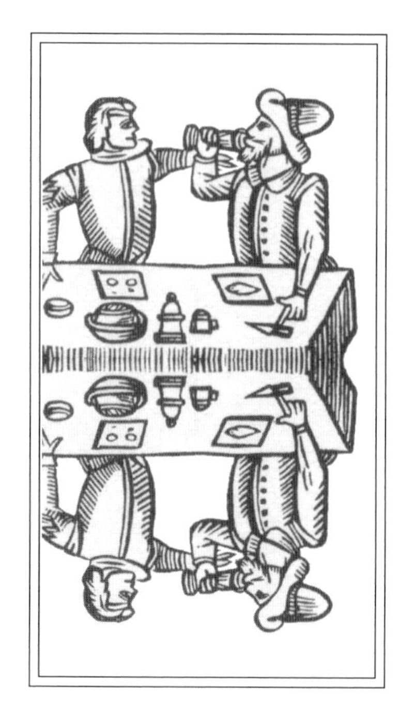

1599
A violent storm struck Barnstaple two days before Christmas.

Candlemas

Kindle the Christmas brand, and then
  Till sunset, let it burn;
Which quench'd, then lay it up again
  Till Christmas next return.
Part must be kept wherewith to tend
  The Christmas log next year,
And where 'tis safely kept, the fiend
  Can do no mischief there.[6]

1652 The Water Poet and Christmas under the Commonwealth

In the middle of the seventeenth century John Taylor, the water-poet and former Royalist, visited Devon at Christmas.[7] Under the Commonwealth the traditional observation of Christmas was being discouraged. Taylor wrote that 'Certain hot, zealous brethren were of opinion that from the 24th of December at night, till the 7th of January following, plum pudding was mere Popery, that a collar of brawn was an abomination, that roast beef was anti-Christian, that mince pies were relics of the Woman of Babylon, and a goose, a turkey or a capon were marks of the beast'. In his description he described 'lambswool', the hot spiced ale mixed with roasted apples. Taylor travelled down to the West Country and wrote:

'I will describe one (farmer) for all the rest in Devonshire and Cornwall. The good man with the dame of the house and everybody else were exceeding glad to see me. With all country courtesy and solemnity, I was had into the parlour. There I was placed at the upper end of the table and my company about me. We had good cheer and free welcome and we were merry without music. After dinner we arose from the board and sat by the fire – where the hearth was embroidered all over with roasted apples, piping hot, expecting a bowl of ale for a cooler (which presently was transformed into warm lambswool). Within an hour after we went to church, where a good old minister spoke very reverendly of my Master, Christ, and also he uttered many good speeches concerning me, exciting and exhorting the people to love and unity, one with another, and to extend their charities to the needy and distressed.

After prayers we returned home where we discoursed merrily, without either profaneness or obscenity; supper being ended we went to cards; some sung carols and merry songs (suitable to the times) then the poor labouring hinds and the maid-servants, with the plough-boys, went nimbly to dancing, the poor toiling wretches being all glad of my company because they had little or no sport at all till I came amongst them and therefore they leaped and skipped for joy, singing a catch to the tune of "HEY":

Let's dance and sing, and make good cheer,
For Christmas comes but once a year.

Thus at active games and gambols of hot-cockles, shoeing the wild mare and the like harmless sports, some part of the night was spent; and early in the morning we took our leave of them thankfully; and though we had been thirteen days well entertained, yet the poor people were very unwilling to let me go; so I left them, quite out of hope to have my company for a twelvemonth's space, that, if I were not banished in my absence, they should have my presence again next 25th December, 1653.

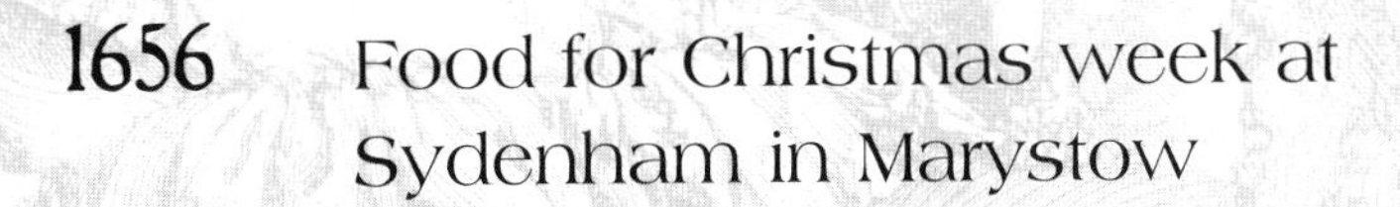

1656 Food for Christmas week at Sydenham in Marystow

One of the few Devon kitchen accounts to survive for the seventeenth century is that of Sir Edward and Lady Arabella Wise for the 1650s. The couple, who were recently married and both in the their early twenties, were in the midst of rebuilding Sydenham, their home in the West Devon parish of Marystow near Tavistock. The rebuilding may have been regretted by later generations of the family: in order to pay for the substantial costs Sir Edward sold his fields just outside Plymouth as common agricultural land but it was shortly afterwards resold and developed as Plymouth Dock. In 1656 the Wise family spent Christmas at Sydenham rather than in London where they lived a considerable part of the year. The cost of their provisions over the holiday period exceeded the annual income of an ordinary Devon labourer.

The list of food they consumed is interesting to compare against the description given just three years previously by John Taylor of his Westcountry Christmas. Sir

Edward and Lady Arabella had an ox especially killed for the festivities but they also had in the larder other cuts of beef as well as mutton, a roasting pig, cocks, plovers, snipes, geese, capon, ducks, salmon, rabbit, and marrow bones.

There were a number of pies made including woodcock pie, turkey pie, five minced pies and a quince pie. Vegetables were not listed but presumably there were carrots, parsnips, turnips and cabbages as these were commonly ground throughout Devon. Among the herbs were rosemary and bay. There was also a considerable portion of butter, milk and eggs and sweet tarts and pies were baked. In the previous week jumbals (a type of cake), jelly and biscuits were made, presumably some for Christmas. These were flavoured with apples, prunes, currants, raisings, nutmeg and 'spicery'. Finally there were many bottles of wine (white, Canary and claret were particularly mentioned) and more than five hogsheads of ale and beer.[8] The amount of food suggests that Christmas at Sydenham with the Wise family was similar to that described by John Taylor a few years before.

1725 Predictions for an early Georgian Christmas morning in Exeter

From the pen of Andrew Brice, Exeter's prolific writer and publisher, came this account of Christmas which was printed in his own newspaper, *Brice's Weekly Journal*. The lines must have scandalised the city.

Predictions, &c for Christmas Morning

The Town Clocks have now proclaimed the full-grown Age of Night: and Woe to you peaceful Inhabitants, whose lodging Apartments front the troubled Streets! In vain shall you invoke kind Morpheus with his leaden fingers to close your heavy eyelids! For lo! The roving Hydra, with all his numerous and increasing mouths, will invade the avenues of your ears! But hark! The melodious Orpheus has, by his cogent Strains and Harmony, set all the beasts a-dancing, to celebrate the new-born Festival; and whose skillful Hand makes the very Stones, Pot-sherds, and rotten Turnips, caper as high as your very Windows. But say, ye knowing Planets, whose twinkling eyes discern all things below, proceed the Base Notes from the Musician's powerful Chords, or are they the hoarse murmurings of Bruin, rampant with his ragged staff? Pho! How one's senses may be deceived in the gloominess of Night! I discern him plain. A comical mistake; ha, ha, ha! It's only Daddy with his Bassoon. Oh! are you there with your bears? I know you are now; the city mew-sick, and the Suburb Mobility at their Heels, hopping the Cow's courant to the tune of the 100 Psalm. Ha, ha, ha! Well, pass ye on; and prepare your instruments to play on the bones of a piping hot surloin; making way for the various sets of vocal choristers, who in their turns claim audience.

Come Captain Avery and Goss, where are you? Come, open your stinking throats, leave off swearing, hold your lanterns not too near your ugly stranguery faces, and strike up a carol. Hold! hold! enough! too much a conscience! Pax on your insufferable clamours! Not an Hum more of your confounded brawling, lest you have the contents of twenty full-charged chamber-vessels thrown upon your heads in the warbling of a Quaver! Ten whiffs more of your tobacco breaths would taint all the good cheer in the neighbourhood.

Whose there? Liny? – Well, rosin thy bow with a candle-end, and play a sonata of thy own making, such a piece as would dash Mr W– on himself out of countenance, should he be desired but to imitate ir... Oh! You sun of a

W...! This is ten times worse that the abominable Strum-strum of a Spaniard's Guitar under his Dulcinea's Window. Go, scamper home quickly, or Sirtah, you'll bring a Congregation of Cats upon your back, for making such a cursed vile Scraping on the guts of one of their deceased fellows.

Hark! I believe these approaching are a new set. Listen a little: perhaps these may afford something more grateful... But oh! For a peal of thunder, or at least a Triple-salvo like as from Tower Hill, to drown the hideous growling! Had the Shepherds been your Auditors, instead of the heavenly melody, they had fled to Bethlehem, not with joy, but for fear of being devoured with their flocks by an army of wolves.

But thanks to the destinies for some relief! Cousin Tom draws nigh; and when the sun arises the moon and stars must set. Pies in you, Cousin! Why don't you sue for a patent, that none may have the liberty to break people's sleep but yourself. Why do you suffer such a parcel of noisy interlopers to take the drink out of your mouth? Come, we ever expect some new composure of your own from you, some mercy touch after Joseph and Mary with travelling are weary, to divert us who are not a whit less tired than themselves... Well done, I protest! This is as good as Punch's Jigg after the doleful Puppet Tragedy of the harmless Children in the Wood: and may he not have a merry Christmas, say I, who refuses to drop at least a graceful Tester into your Box!

But the time of Matins is happily coming on, and the banging of stalls in some measure also begins to cease. Tho' the frequent carols scarce influence any to give glory in the highest, yet many strolling females are inclined to show their goodwills towards men. One just arrived to the years of Puberty, having heard some modern gallants say they'd rather have the p.. then the itch, resolves to venture one, rather than longer endure the other. Some bumble maids (thro' a false imitation of that Virtue praised in the songs aforesaid) patiently submit to their burthen, which they think but light, in a place even inferior to a stall; planting themselves perhaps in the very bulk where another just before had watered.

A notorious Holland-trader, who had long been suspected of clandestine taking up of linen, like to be catched, between the hours of 5 and 6, in the very act of smuggling.

The tuneful cocks seem to imitate the swan, sing their own mournful elegies, and give mutual warning, of their approaching fate. Alas, poor Chanticleer! Must thou, whose awful voice and majestic port make the

1607

Plymouth's lead pipes burst in the severe winter weather.

1608

Barumites walked across the frozen river Taw at Barnstaple.

1628

Sixteen braces of rabbits were purchased for Forde House in Newton Abbot on Christmas Eve.

undaunted king of beasts so tremble; must thou, whose matchless labour should inspire a very coward with never yielding courage, in a lawful generous engagement; must thou, who so lately, strutting in thy seraglio of beauteous and obedient shoes, gavest the breeding dames, better content than Alcides ever could boast of; must thou, whose opportune and shrill alarms could rouse the drowsy husband and sluggish servant to their neglected duties; thou, whose prolific genitoirs helped so amply to provide not only eggs but poultry for this tide of festivity; must even thou, alas! be bound worse than a galley-slave, hampered like a perjured witness, forgerer or cheat, to be insulted, abused, battered and lastly murdered by the hands of mischievous boys, lubberly hostlers, and bloody butchers? Is this the reward of thy many noble qualities, to undergo greater punishment for thy services and virtues than is often inflicted on the greatest delinquent or capital offender? Indignity without a match! Yet take comfort however in this thou are herein a grand example of patience to the best and most deserving of men who suffer persecutions. As a man falleth before wicked men, so fallest thou... But hold your hands, ye more than savages, ye worse than brutes. Consider, that every fatal stroke may perhaps make a dozen widows mourn. And O ye Belchians, (if any of you chance to sojurn here) can ye stand tamely by, and see your first instructors in your noble science of offence, from whom you learned the genteel beautifying art of snick or snee, suffer such unworthy, vile, ungrateful treatment? For shame, pluck your idle hands out of your greasy pockets, and rescue the brave, distressed heroes from the merciless barbarians! Tell the cruel wretches, their abominable practice is a scandal to foreign nations, even the more Christian Turks; and as Exeter exceeds therein all parts of the kingdom, the cruel toleration, if continued, will reflect not a little shame on parents and masters, tho' not on magistrates.

Two maudlin religionists at an alehouse, who never trouble church or meeting with their company, in their zeal forgetting their house and bec, maintain dispute for more than 13 (not glasses but quarts) in defence of their different opinions. The Dissenter tenaciously holds his own, till he disgorges it with his ale in the face of his antagonist; and the other champ on swears lustily to stand by the church... till he drops asleep under the table.

The Six a clock bell begins to toll. Betty Wagtail steals slyly from the 'Prentice's bed to unmake her own, before she dares venture out to Morning Prayer.

At Seven those who lie steeped in the fancied Sweets of unlawful pleasures, like flies in a treacle-barrel, begin to rouse up and shake themselves like Sampson rising from the lap of Delilah, lest the Phillistines should come upon them.

Day light appears when many who have watched all night not caring for the double duty of likewise praying by day, reel home to bed to snore out the hours they ought to employ at church.

Greater hacking of roast pork and beef about the hours of 8 and 9, than committed by the Duke of Berwick's Troopers and Dragoons at the Battle of Almanza.

Many devout countenances may be seen in several congregations about 10 and 11, but whose souls pant greatly after the savoury provision at their kitchen fires.

P... on the Philistines dispatches his text as dexterously as a hungry judge does a doubtful cause, lest his full dressed dinner should be spoiled.

Greater vigour and courage will be shown at one a clock, by several moroding parties, in storming goose-castles, covered ways of giblets, and redoubts of chicken, than every appeared in the main body of confederates, in attacking the outworks of the enemy in Flanders. Nor will the Eating Army think they have their bellies full, half so soon as did the Fighters.

Cum multis a iis, which I've neither room nor inclination at present to insert.[9]

1738 England's earliest recorded mummers' play

1630
A Newton Abbot buttery boy received 12 shillings and 6 pence for his quarterly wages.

Exeter's Andrew Brice also wrote a short, but what is thought to be the earliest, manuscript description[10] of a Mummers' Play.

At Christmas are (or at least very lately were) fellows wont to go about from House to House in Exeter amumming; one of whom in a (borrowed) Holland shirt most gorgeously be-ribboned, over his waistcoat, &c flourishing a faulchion, very valiantly entertaining the admiring spectators thus

> Oh! Here comes I Saint George, a man of courage bold
> And with my spear I winn'd three Crowns of Gold.
> I slew the Dragon, and brought him to the Slaughter.
> And by that very means I married Sabra, the beauteous King of Egypt's daughter.
>
> Play Music.[11]

1643
The Christmas provisions at Tawstock Court in North Devon included cloves, liquorice, cinnamon, ginger, prunes, syrup of mulberries and a six-pound jar of almonds.

1644
Observance of Christmas is discouraged: the making of plum puddings and mince pies forbidden.

1793/1893 'Jasper Berryman's Christmas party' by H. Skinner

The following story was set by H. Skinner in the late eighteenth century and written for *The Exeter Flying Post* in 1893.

Jasper Berryman's Christmas Party: A Legend of Old Exeter[12]

Twas in the year 1793, exactly one hundred years ago this very Christmas, that the little episode we are about to relate took place. The winter of that year had set in with unusual severity. The Exe was frozen over from Head Weir to Trew's Weir, and everybody was looking forward to spending a jolly Christmas and having a bit of fun on the ice.

It was late in the afternoon of Christmas Eve, that the last of the goods and chattles of the undertaker, Jasper Berryman, were heaped into a wagon, and a pair of lean horses dragged the conveyance along for the fourth time from Trinity Lane to Mary Arches Lane, for to the latter street the undertaker was removing with all his household. Having closed his old shop, he nailed a notice to the door, to the effect that the premises were to be sold or let, and started off on foot to his new abode.

He was, not unnaturally, in somewhat depressed spirits, when turning his back finally on his old home, and approaching the little yellow house, which had so long taken his fancy (being near the cemetery). Having crossed the threshold and finding his new abode in great confusion he sighed at the recollection of his old hovel, where during eighteen years everything had been conducted with the strictest regularity, and he scolded his daughters and the maid-of-all-work for their dilatoriness and set to work to assist them himself.

Order was soon established; the grandfather's clock, the dresser with the crockery, the table and sofa, occupied the corners assigned to them in the back room; in the front room was placed the master's handiwork, which consisted of coffins of all sizes and shapes; and the cupboards were filled with mourning cloaks and torches. Over the door appeared a signboard, representing a corpulent cupid holding a reversed torch, with the inscription:

Here are sold
and ornamented
plain and covered coffins
coffins are also let out
on hire
and old ones repaired.

Although the signboard has long since disappeared, this old house may still be recognised by its carved brackets and overhanging windows. The girls retired to their room, and Jasper, having inspected his dwelling, sat down by the window and ordered the tea to be prepared.

The enlightened reader is aware that both Shakespeare and Sir Walter Scott represented their grave-diggers as cheerful and jocose persons, in order to arouse our imagination more forcibly by the contrast between the disposition of the worker and the character of his work. Out of regard to truth, however, we cannot follow their example, and are compelled to admit that the disposition of our undertaker fully corresponded with his mournful calling. Jasper Berryman was habitually sullen and thoughtful. His silence might occasionally be broken for the sole purpose of scolding his daughters when he chanced to find them idle, gazing out of windows at the passers-by, or asking an exorbitant price for his goods, of those who had the misfortune (and sometimes also the good fortune) to require them.

Thus it happened that Jasper, now sipping his fourth cup of tea, was as usual sunk in melancholy reflections. He thought of the pouring rain which fell at the very outset of the retired Brigadier's funeral the previous week. Many mourning cloaks had shrunk in consequence, and many hats spoiled. He foresaw unavoidable expenditure, for his old stock of mourning attire had fallen into a pitiful condition. He hoped to charge a good round sum for the funeral of the merchant Reddaway's old wife, who had now been nearly a year at death's door. But the old woman lay dying at Lympstone, and Berryman feared lest her heirs would neglect to send for him all that distance, and would come to terms with a nearer undertaker. These meditations were unexpectedly disturbed by three freemason-like taps at the door.

'Who is there?' asked Berryman.

The door opened and a man in whom the shoemaker was recognised at a glance, walked in, and cheerfully approached.

'Pardon me, good master Berryman' said he 'pardon my intruding upon you – I was anxious to make your acquaintance. I am a bootmaker, my name is Nat Treadwell, and I live across the street, and thinking you were not exactly settled, I came to ask you and your daughters with us in a friendly way.'

The invitation was accepted with good will. The undertaker asked the bootmaker to sit down and take a cup of tea, and, thanks to the cordial disposition of Nathan Treadwell, their conversation soon became friendly.

'How does your trade prosper?' asked Jasper.

'Ah– he– he–!' answered Treadwell, 'so, so, I cannot complain, although my goods are of course different from yours: a live man can do without boots, but a dead man cannot do without a coffin.'

'Very true' remarked Jasper: 'however, if a live man has not got wherewith to pay for his boots, one cannot take it amiss in him if he goes barefooted, but a dead beggar has a coffin gratis.'

In this manner they conversed for some time. At last the bootmaker rose and taking leave of the undertaker, renewed his invitation.

The next day at one o'clock precisely, the undertaker and his daughters passed through the wicket of the newly-bought house on their way to neighbour Treadwell. The small dwelling of the bootmaker was filled with guests, who chiefly consisted of little tradesmen their wives, and their workmen, with a few others including Dan Tucker, one of the old city watchmen (there were no policemen in those days) who had, in spite of his calling, managed to secure the special goodwill of his host.

1656

The Christmas provisions at Sydenham House in West Devon included six ducks, four geese, one rabbit, three turkeys, one roasting pig and twenty-four chickens.

1681
Mary Christmas was buried at Barnstaple on 21 January.

Almost everybody in Exeter knew old Dan. Jasper hastened to make his acquaintance as he would that of a man of whom he might stand in need, sooner or later, and when the guests took their seats at dinner, they sat next each other. Mr and Mrs Treadwell and their daughter Penelope, who had seen but seventeen summers, whilst dining with and entertaining their guests, assisted the cook to wait upon them. Jars of beer were fetched from the alehouse at the bottom of the street, and influenced by the good cheer, Tucker ate for four, but although Jasper did not cede to him, his daughters observed a stricter ceremony.

The conversation was becoming louder and louder, when suddenly the host begged for a few moments' attention, and drawing the cork of a bottle of 'Old Tom' exclaimed in a loud voice 'My Friends, a Merry Christmas and the health of my good Louisa!' The bottle passed freely, and the host tenderly kissed the fresh face of his forty-year-old helpmate, while the guests drank noisily to the health of the good Louisa.

'The health of my amiable guests!' exclaimed the host opening another bottle. And his guests thanked him, and again drained their glasses. Then toast followed upon toast; the health of each guest was drunk separately; they toasted Exeter; they toasted Topsham and nearly all other Devonshire towns in general, and each one in particular; they drank to masters; they drank to foremen. Jasper drank sedulously; and was so elated, that he himself proposed some jocular toast, and even went so far as to kiss Penelope under the mistletoe.

Suddenly, one of the guests, a baker, raised his glass, and exclaimed, 'To the health of those we work for!' This proposal, like all the others, was joyously and unanimously applauded. The guests saluted each other the tailor, bowed to the bootmaker, the bootmaker to the tailor, the baker to both; all to the baker and so on. Dan Tucker in the midst of those mutual salutations, exclaimed, turning to his neighbour.

'What now! drink, sir, to the health of thy dead ones! All laughed, but the undertaker considering himself affronted became sullen. Nobody noticed him; the party continued its carouse and it was midnight when all rose from the table. The guests dispersed at a late hour and most of them were elevated. The baker and the bookbinder, whose face appeared as if bound in red Morocco, led the watchman between them to his box, carrying out in this case the maxim 'one good turn deserves another'. The undertaker returned home tipsy and wrathful. 'Why, indeed', reasoned he aloud; 'why is my craft worse than any other? Is an undertaker then, brother to a hangman? What had the heathens to laugh at? Is an undertaker a Christmas harlequin? I meant to have asked them to a house-warming, to have given them a feast, but let them wait till they get it. And I shall now invite, instead, those for whom I work, my orthodox dead.'

'What sir? said the maid, who was pulling off his boots, 'what do'ee talk about. You bain't goint to ax the dead to a housewarming shurely?'

'By – I shall ask them,' continued Jasper, 'I shall ask them at once, for tomorrow. pray come my benefactors and feast with me tomorrow evening; I shall entertain you with what God has given me; So saying the undertaker tumbled into bed, and soon began to snore.

It was still dark when Jasper was roused. The merchant Reddaway's wife had died that very night, and a special messenger had been sent on horseback with this intelligence. The undertaker gave him sixpence for a dram, dressed in haste, took a chaise and drove to Lympstone. The mutes were already stationed at the gates of the house where lay the defunct; tradesmen were going in and out like ravens at their prey. The corpse lay on a table, and relations, neighbourhood friends crowded around. Jasper went up to the merchant's nephew, a young fellow in a fashionable coat, and assured him that the coffin, cloaks, pall, and other funeral furniture would be delivered with all punctuality and without fail. The heir thanked him absently, saying that he would not bargain about he expense, but would trust implicitly to his conscience. The undertaker, as usual, swore that he would not overcharge; exchanged a significant glance with his workmen and started off to make the necessary arrangements.

1727
Three days before Christmas Valentine and Orson *was performed at the New Inn at Exeter.*

The whole day was spent driving to and from between Exeter and Lympstone; towards night, all being arranged, he settled with his driver, and returned homewards on foot. It was a moonlight night.

At the top of South Street, our friend the Watchman was shouting the hour of 'a fine and frosty morning' and on recognising the undertaker wished him good night. It was very late and the old city was as quiet as the grave.

The undertaker was approaching his house, when he suddenly fancied he saw some one ahead of him, open the wicket, pass through and disappear.

'What can this mean? thought Jasper. 'Who is it wants me again? Can it be a thief? Do lovers perhaps visit my silly girls? It bodes evil!' And the undertaker was on the point of running for a watchman to come to his aid.

Just then some other person approached the wicket and was about to enter, but on becoming aware that Jasper was nearing hurriedly, this person stopped, and raised his cocked hat; Jasper fancied he knew the face, but was not, in his haste, able to examine it closely. 'You were coming to me,' said Jasper, breathlessly, 'do me the favour to step in.'

'No ceremony friend,' said the stranger, in a hollow voice, 'walk on, show thy guests the way!'

There was no time to stand on ceremony. The wicket stood open, Jasper went up the staircase, the person following him. Jasper fancied that people were walking about his rooms. 'What devilry is this,' thought he, and hurried in – but here his legs gave way. The room was full of animated corpses. The moon shining through the windows, lit up their yellow and blue faces, sunken mouths, dull half-closed eyes, and thin protruding noses. Jasper recognised in them with dread people who had been buried with his aid; and, in the guest whom he had preceded, a Brigadier who had been interred in the cemetery, a couple of hundred yards off. All the women and men assembled surrounded the undertaker, bowing and

greeting him; all except one poor fellow who carried his head under his arm. He was a pauper and had been buried by Jasper in that fashion through a mistake in the measurement. He seemed shy and ashamed of his tatters and did not venture to come forward, but stood retiredly in a corner. The rest were respectably dressed, the women wore caps with ribbons, those men who had served the State were in uniform, but their faces were unshaven; merchants wore their holiday clothes. 'See'st thou, Berryman,' said the Brigadier in the name of the company, 'how we have all risen at your invitation? Those alone have remained at home who could not possibly come, who had been unable to resist the influences which mother earth set to work upon their frail frames, but even thus, one of them could not rest – so anxious was he to see thee.'

At that moment a small skeleton pushed his way through the crowd and approached Jasper. His skull smiled affectionately at the undertaker, bits of light green and red cloth, and old linen, hung here and there about him, as upon a pole, whilst the bones of his feet rattled in his Hessian boots, like a pestle in a mortar.

'Thou dos'nt recognise me, Berryman' said the skeleton. 'Dosn't thou remember the retired sergeant, Peter Cox, of the Devon Fencibles, the same for whom thou soldest they first coffin in the year '74 – and one of pine for one of oak?' So saying, the corpse extended his bony arms towards him; but Jasper, mastering all his strength, cried out, and pushed him from him. Peter Cox tottered, fell, and went to pieces.

A murmur of indignation was heard amongst the dead; they stood up for the honour of their companion, threatening and upbraiding Jasper; and the poor host, deafened by their cries, and almost pressed to death, losing his presence of mind, fell across the bones of the retired sergeant of the Fencibles and became unconscious. The sunlight had long been streaming across the bed on which the undertaker was sleeping. At last he opened his eyes, and saw before him the maid, blowing the fire. He was silent, expecting the girl to commence the conversation, and to relate to him the result of last night's adventures.

'How thee hast overslept thyself Jasper Berryman, sir,' said Ruth handing him his dressing-gown. 'They neighbours, the tailor and the watchman, came asking thee to come out as it was Boxing Day, but thee was pleased to sleep and we did not like to wake'ee.'

'And did they come to me from the late Mrs Reddaway?'

'Late! Is her daid then?'

'Fool! that thou art! did'st not thou thyself help me to arrange things for her funeral.'

'Have'ee lost thee senses, sir? or ain't'ee got over last night's fuddle? What funeral was there yesterday? Thee did'st feast at the shoemaker's all day, and coming home tipsy, did'st throw thyself on thy bed, and has't slept until this very hour!'

'Indeed,' said the rejoiced undertaker.

'Of course,' answered Ruth.

'Well if that is the case, let me have some milk. And do you run down to the corner and get a quartern of rum. I am awful shaky and feel half dead; and I want a different sort of corpse-reviver to that I had last night.

1799 'A Christmas Carol' by Samuel Taylor Coleridge

Ottery St Mary's most famous writer wrote the following poem at the age of 27 in 1799.

The Shepherds went their hasty way,
And found the lowly stable-shed
Where the Virgin Mary lay:
And now they checked their eager tread,
For to the Babe, that at her bosom clung
A mother's song the Virgin Mother sung.

They told her how a glorious light,
Streaming from a heavenly throng,
Around them shone, suspending night!
While sweeter than a mother's song,
Blest Angels heralded the Saviour's birth,
Glory to God on high! And Peace on Earth.

She listened to the tale divine,
And closer still the Babe she prest;
And while she cried, the Babe is mine!
The milk rushed faster to her breast:
Joy rose within her, like a summer's morn;
Peace, Peace on Earth! The Prince of Peace is born.

Thou mother of the Prince of Peace,
Poor, simple and of low estate!
That strife should vanish, battle cease,
O why should this thy soul elate?
Sweet music's loudest note, the poet's story –
Didst thou ne'er love to hear of fame and glory?

And is not War a youthful king
A stately hero clad in mail?
Beneath his footsteps laurels spring;
Him Earth's majestic monarch's hail
Their friend, their playmate! And his bold bright eye
Compels the maiden's love-confessing sigh.

'Tell this in some more courtly scene,
To maids and youths in robes of state!
I am a woman poor and mean,
And therefore is my soul elate.
War is a ruffian, all with guilt defiled,
That from their aged father tears his child!

'A murderous fiend, by fiends adored,
He kills the sire and starves the son;
The husband kills, and from her board
Steals all his widow's toil had won;
Plunder's God's world of beauty; rends away
All safety from the night, all comfort from the day.

'Then wisely is my soul elate
That strife should vanish, battle cease:
I'm poor and of a low estate,
The Mother of the Prince of Peace.
Joy rises in me, like a summer's morn:
Peace, Peace on Earth! The Prince of Peace is born'.[13]

1728
Hamlet *was performed by the Company of Comedians a few days before Christmas.*

1787
Easterly winds were thought to be responsible for more than a hundred Dartmouth vessels not returning from Newfoundland.

1789
Three days before Christmas 21 convicts were taken from Exeter to be transported on the Dolphin *for Botany Bay.*

1813 'The Year' by John Bidlake of Plymouth

The following verses form part of a longer poem on the year written by John Bidlake, school master at Plymouth, in 1813.

Tis now the hallowed time, sacred to Him,
Who brought on earth good will and peace to man;
Who in a mortal form, despised, forlorn,
A man of sorrows, came to teach a world
Corrupt, the bliss of pure benevolence,
To teach men how to conquer sin and death,
And ope'd the gates of everlasting life.

Warned by religious awe, awe soon forgot,
The shrivelled miser spreads his scanty hand,
Nor from his rust-worn gate awhile he spurns
The poor and wandering train; the gate beset,
By mastiffs huge and grim, and churlish frowns;
His few saved farthings pay the unwilling debt
Of charity, which he allows as due
To Heaven for all the year. But cheered by those
Whose larger bounty glads the bitter hour,
And bids the furrowed face of poverty
Assume a transient smile; the wretched train
Of Indigence now share the season's joy;
Now taste the luxury of one full meal,
And see the chimney blaze with a generous warmth.

Now Hospitality, to cheer the gloom
Of winter, invitation sends abroad;
The rural housewife lays the annual block
Of Christmas on the hearth; and bids a blaze
Of tenfold brightness glad its sable spot;
Then sprucely decks the windows with fresh sprigs
Of ever-greens, triumphant o'er the storms
Of fading time, while ever social mirth
And rival kindness, loads the smoking board;
And boisterous sport, and heavy dance resound.
With verdant honours too, the sexton decks
The pews, and shares the universal joy:
The holy priest he clothes in purer white;
And solemn hymns proclaims the sleepless eve
Of this auspicious day, so dear to man.[14]

1814 A masquerade ball in Regency Exeter

On December 27 1814 Mrs Hewett hosted a Grand Ball and Masquerade at her home in Colleton Crescent in Exeter. The row of houses, perched high over the river Exe, was newly-built and would have been a fashionable address to attend a Christmas Masquerade Ball. It was reported in *Trewman's Exeter Flying-Post* that the ball comprised:

a large number of the principal fashionables of this city and its neighbourhood. The company began to assemble at eight o'clock, and continued to increase until eleven, at which time between 2 and 3 hundred persons were present. The Ball Room was fitted up with much taste; it was decorated with festoons of flowers in the most elegant and fanciful style; and the floor was prettily chalked, giving to the *tout ensemble* a very pleasing effect. Dancing commenced about eleven, and continued till half past twelve, when the supper rooms were opened, the tables of which displayed a profusion of delicacies, laid out with taste and elegance, to refresh and enliven the motley assemblage. Everything which the season could produce was served up with the greatest hospitality; the sweet meats and wines were excellent; vivacity and good humour reigned triumphant; and indeed, the whole went off admirably. The party separated about five o'clock, all highly delighted with their evening's entertainment, and most particularly with the polite attention, which was shown by the lady of the house to every one of her numerous guests. The following are characters which were particularly conspicuous, being each of them well supported.

A group of Indians, a Doctor Syntax, a Jew Peddler and his wife, a Turk, a Scaramouch, two Pantaloons, a Oyster Woman, a mendicant Friar, a Nun, A Major Sturgeon, a Jerry and Mrs Sneak, a Sir Geoffrey Jealous of the Year 1765, a Miss Lucretia Mac Tab, a Devonshire Farmer, a Seller of Gingerbread, a Magician, a Gypsy Fortune Teller, three Barristers, a Doctor Ollapod, a Country Boy, a Housemaid, several Flower Girls, Fruit Girls, etc. with lots of Dominoes.

1792
Sixty schoolchildren were treated to a Christmas dinner at Honiton.

1798
A lion, lioness and elephant were on view at the Crown & Sceptre in Exeter.

1799
The Ethalion *was wrecked on the Saint's Rocks and the crew saved by the* Nimrod *and* Sylph.

1803
A great storm blew through Devon on Christmas Day.

1816 Christmas provisions at Castle Hill near South Molton

The Christmas kitchen account for the Fortescue family at Castle Hill in 1816 shows a very high level of expenditure. The family, like other members of the aristocracy and gentry, were by convention bound to provide for the poor at Christmas and undoubtedly some of the provisions, particularly the hundreds of pounds of meat, were spent on meals for them. But the family itself also enjoyed suitable food and drink: at a Christmas meal a few years later they drank a bottle of port and another of sherry between them and only a few guests.

Kitchen account, 1816, from December the 20th to the 27th

693 lbs of beef from the farm
113 lbs of mutton
77½ pounds of veal
a roasting pig
fish (whiting and codfish)
2 fowls
1 duck
1 turkey
16 lbs of butter
12 quarts of milk
2½ pints of cream
30 eggs
6 lbs of currants
4 lbs of raisins
2 lumps of sugar
moist sugar
4 bags of potatoes
1 bag of turnips

total cost £21 11s ½d [15]

1820s Late Georgian Exeter

James Cossins, an Exeter man, reminisced in 1877 about his life in the city some fifty years before. His memories were that:

The Choirs of various churches would go round the parishes on Christmas Eve, stopping at the principal houses to sing an appropriate anthem or a Christmas carol; this over, the loudest tenor voice would call out the names of the nearest residents, such as 'Good morning, Mr Snugg; good morning Mrs Snugg, and the young Snuggs, past three o'clock; a very cold and frosty morning.' or the snow is falling fast. The young reader must understand, in those days, the winters were much more severe than now; skating almost a certainty, and snow falling at various times for two or three days, and remaining on the ground for several weeks. I have seen birds lying dead on the ground for want of food. My father informed me that the snow had been so high on Haldon that men were sent from Exeter to cut a passage through it, to allow the mails to pass.

Returning to the perambulation, the choir consisted of singers, accompanied by a fiddle or two, bass viol, a clarinet or flute. The above named instruments were used in churches that had no organ. On the rounds some parties were waiting the arrival of the choir with a cup of tea, coffee or soup which was very acceptable. A good efficient choir would be accompanied by lots of 'camp followers' who rendered assistance by carrying chairs, lanterns, &c, also by holding the music in front of the performers. About six o'clock the various rounds were finished; at half-past six the Cathedral bell tolled out, the front doors were opened, and then there was a great rush of people, about half filling the nave, many in a state that indicated that they were not members of the temperance society, being very noisy, and smoking. This conduct not meeting the approval of the Dean and Chapter they ceased to have the nave opened some years since. At seven o'clock the organist played the Old Hundredth Psalm on the 'Great Organ' the chorister boys singing from the 'Minstrels' Gallery' which was lit up with candles. The morning and afternoon services were thinly attended, but a great many outsiders went to hear the anthem. The parish churches were well-attended in the morning, afternoon scarcely anyone present, evening three or four churches open, and these very thinly attended. So universal was the social and family gathering, that the High Street in the evening had an appearance of a deserted town, with respect to people moving about.

Now for family meetings on Christmas days. 'Grandfather' would, if possible, invite the whole of his family descendants, including grandchildren, to partake of what the festive table produced, which generally speaking, consisted of a goose, beef and a large smoked ham &c, followed by a huge fig pudding covered with white sugar to correspond with the snow-clad roofs. Beer was not forgotten, good home-brewed October twelve months was tapped by the landlords for their customers. Dinner over, chairs were placed in a semi-circle around the blazing fire, children sitting in front or on the knee, and the topic of conversation would be old family times, absent friends and passing events until about five o'clock, when the old ladies' delight, a good cup of tea with a little bit of green in it, was announced. After this ceremony, which occupied about an hour, cards were introduced; the family game, two pence half penny loo was played until supper time, nine o'clock. The coin was put in the snuffer tray; a cup or small basin called the 'pitcher' was also placed in the centre of the table, the holder of the ace of trumps depositing a half penny in it, the amount being divided amongst the younger branches. After supper, again sitting round the ashen faggot fire, healths and toasts were proposed, and good old seasonable and patriotic songs sand until about midnight. Then came the trying time of departure, with respect to children, some

sleepy, others crying. Before leaving, a hint was given that the ham would be nice and solid about eleven the following day. 'Oh yes, I understand, you are all welcome. Now mind I shall expect you.' This led to another family day's enjoyment.

There was another prominent incident in those parties, the maternal head-dress, net caps, the polls about three inches high, lace trimmings, interspersed with various coloured ribbons. This piece of gear having to last the season, the different milliners' tastes were well scrutinized. Hair fronts, too, were worn across forehead, according to taste either plain or dangling curls, nicely put out of hand by the barber. This paraphernalia was pinned up in a white handkerchief and carried with great care through the streets which was an intimation that 'I am going to a party'. No doubt the reader will think why this show off, but the people had not the convenience of cabs then as now. Sedan chairs were the only conveyances available. In 1823, Humphrey Stark started four pair-horse hackney coaches; now we have about one hundred cabs and flies. That assistants in shops might have an opportunity of spending a few hours with their friends on Christmas eve, shutters were put up about six o'clock, continuing a little later each evening until New Year's eve.

Another even not notice now was Old Christmas Eve, on the 5th January, when confectioners tried to excel each other in their art. The streets were crowded with parents and children visiting the various shops; the outsiders were more numerous by hundreds than buyers. Another Christmas pastime, but one scarcely known to the present generation, was the 'mummers', who would visit private houses, and ask permission to perform before the assembled company. The different characters were generally well got up, and the parts very creditably performed. For this a liberal collection was made, and some of the good things of the table presented to the players. It was customary at some of the inns at this season to invite the 'landlord's' customers and friends to supper, and have a bowl of punch, etc. I will give one instance of it which was at the Barnstaple Inn, North Street, kept by Mr Ireland. After supper the guests, numbering from thirty to fifty, would, if convenient, adjourn to the large kitchen, which was nicely decorated. The chairman and vice with their yards of clay occupied seats on each side of the fire place, with a huge ashen faggot burning; on this occasion they were named 'Gog and Magog', it being in the 'pattern parish' of St David's. Mr Carpenter, the organist with the elder portion of the choir, added to the musical department by singing glees, catches, duets, and songs; other parties filling up the interval with toasts, songs, or recitations, and a very pleasant enjoyable evening was spent. Those who had no domestic ties would remain until the small hours, when the kind host and hostess would bring around tea and coffee. Such were the incidents of bygone days, and to those whose memory goes back to that old time, no doubt the foregoing remarks will bring to mind many happy hours spent, many sincere friends, and many good old citizens.[16]

1820s The Yule Log and Wassailing

The Reverend Daniel Lysons and his brother Samuel described Devon's Christmas customs in the 1820s. They wrote that 'the Yule or Christmas log is still burnt on Christmas eve in some parts of the county; they have a custom of burning, on Christmas eve, a large faggot of green ash. Mummers go about at the Christmas season in some parts of the county, acting a kind of rude drama, on the subject of the exploits of St George'. According to the two brothers the ceremonial toasting of apple orchards was still then very prevalent in Devon. They wrote:

In most parts of the cider district a custom still prevails, of what was called in ancient times 'wassailing' the apple trees. This custom was accompanied by the superstitious belief, in the words of an old poet,

The more or less fruit they will bring,
As you do give them wassailing.

Robert Herrick, *Hesperides*

This ceremony at some places is performed on Christmas Eve; in others, on Twelfth Day Eve. It consists in drinking a health to one of the apple-trees, with wishes for its good bearing, which generally turns out successful, as the best bearing tree in the orchard is selected for the purpose. It is attended with singing some verses applicable to the occasion, beginning, 'Health to thee, good apple tree'. The potation consists of cider, in which is put roasted apples or toast: when all have drank, the remainder of the contents of the bowl are sprinkled over the apple tree. The old Saxon term 'wassail' (in some parts of the county they now call it *watsail*, and apply it to drinking) which is well known to imply drinking of health, is thus defined in the glossary to the Exmoor dialect: 'A drinking song sung on Twelfth Day Eve, throwing toast to the apple trees in order to have a fruitful year, which seems to be a relic of the heathen sacrifice to Pomona'.[17]

1804

The tragedy 'Mahomet' was performed by the boys of Mr Weatherdon's Academy in Newton Abbot just before Christmas.

1805

On Christmas the Admiral Cornwallis *sailed out of Plymouth in search of French naval ships.*

1806

On Boxing Day a marine was flogged in Torbay for robbery.

1820s Mummers in Exeter

It was claimed in 1883 that the custom of Mummers in Exeter had died out. One writer, only identified by the initials 'G.T.', noted of 'Christmas Pastimes in Exeter Sixty Years Ago' that:

Railways, penny newspapers, telegrams, and the 'wondrous brain-power' of political leaders in these days have annihilated most of the old customs indulged in by our forefathers. 'The Mummers' were an institution recognised at Christmas time. A few lads occupied their spare time after leaving work, towards Christmas, in preparing for the heroic drama of St George. The 'getting up' was not such as Mr

1809
Mary Dondeswill, a native of Devon who travelled the county as a beggar, died at Glastonbury at the age of, it was alleged, 110.

1810
The Henry *was wrecked in Plymouth Sound.*

1811
A few days before Christmas several hundred French prisoners left Dartmoor for Stapleton Prison.

Planche would approve of, or the dialogue such as would pass muster before even the humblest critic of the modern drama. 'The Mummers' did not seek criticism so much as coppers.

> If unmelodious was their song,
> It was a hearty note and strong.
> Who lists may in their mumming see
> Traces of ancient mystery;
> White shirts supplied the masquerade,
> And smutted cheeks the visors made.

The septuagenarian of Exeter will well remember these old 'mummers' traversing the streets at Christmas time, in all their finery of white shirts, white trousers, ribbons, swords, and buckles, performing, as they did, in the various public-houses, and in such private houses as they could command attention from; and in the country also, from the baronial hall to the farmhouse kitchen, they always had a cordial welcome, commencing at Christmas Eve, the ashen faggot saturnalia.

> 'When old Christmas brought his sports again.'

The exploits of the favourite saint of England, St George, and his destruction of the mighty Turk, formed the prominent feature of this household drama.

Probably it was a remnant of the old miracle plays of the Middle Ages, and represented the triumph of Christianity over paganism. The principal characters were St George, the Turkish Knight, old Father Christmas, old Dol Dorothy, and the Doctor. Latterly, some rather incongruous additions were made – as the Duke of Wellington, Blucher and Napoleon, probably arising out of a patriotic feeling after the battle of Waterloo.

In the performance, Father Christmas thus introduced the party:

> 'Here come I, old Father Christmas, welcome, or welcome not,
> I hope old Father Christmas will never be forgot.
> Room, room, brave gallants, give us room!
> We've come to show our acting on this Christmas time!'

Then St George comes forward with the following bouncing announcement:

> 'Here comes I, St George, the valiant Knight,
> To slay the Turkish Knight I'm come to fight.
> 'Twas I that brought the Dragon to the slaughter,
> And won the King of Egypt's fairest daughter.'

This is followed by the response of the Turkish Knight, who says:

> 'Here comes I, the Turkish Knight,
> From the Turkish land to fight,
> I'll fight St George, with courage bold,
> And if his blood be hot, I'll make it cold'.

A fight then ensues, after stage-fighting fashion, and the Turkish Knight falls. Sometimes Bonaparte also attacks St George, and of course also falls. St George then ruefully contemplates his fallen foes and says:

> 'These men have had some deep and deadly wounds,
> I fear they'll never wish to fight again.'
> And then compassionately enquires for a doctor:
> 'Is there a doctor to be found,
> who can cure these men of their deep and deadly wound?'

The doctor steps forward – a quack of superlative skill and excellence – who looks upon the prostrate men and replies:

> 'Yes, St George, there is a doctor to be found,
> Able to cure these men of their deep and deadly wound.'
> St George: 'What are thy travels, Doctor?'
> Doctor: 'Sir, I've travelled through Italy, Ireland, Germany and Spain,
> And if these champions' heads are off, I'll put them on again'.
> St George: 'Try thy skill, Doctor.'

Doctor feels pulse, looks grave, administers a celebrated pill, and gradually the patients rise, recover their feet, and retire, accompanied by other byplay, speeches, and rhymes, followed by the necessary routine of the collecting-box. The dialogue and acting of the Christmas pieces appears to have varied from time to time, and it would be difficult to obtain a correct rendering of the original story. Like our old favourite, *Punch*, additions and improvements have been made from time to time, which find acceptance by a not too critical audience. A spirited sketch by Stockdale of the 'Mummer' performance in an old farmhouse kitchen is given in the *Illustrated London News* of Christmas, 1850, of which the descriptive letter-press runs thus – 'Hark! What shout is that?' – on which confusion seizes all – men, women and children rushing pell-mell, scrambling to the highest bench 'The Mummers are coming, hurrah!' And then entered six or seven youths fantastically bedecked with ribbons and gay, antiquated garments, ransacked from the bureaus of old dames; here and there a bright silken bow, worn as a favour from their own dear Marys. Space being cleared, the play representing the unconquerable of old England partially attracts the attention of the noisy audience. A warrior, lip corked *a la moustache*, personating the ambitious Napoleon, is brought to encounter St George, who after a fierce combat lays the vaunting Gallic dead upon the earth, the wall echoing the boisterous applause that greets his downfall. However, by the interposition of old Father Christmas, he is restored to partake again of the season's blessings.

The *Illustrated News* for December 1866, in an article on 'Christmas Mummers in

1812

The Levant *arrived in Plymouth from Belfast with a cargo of skins.*

1813

Counterfeit three-shilling tokens were circulating through Devon.

1814

Three days after Christmas Exmouth's lifeboat was carried away by a high tide.

1815

The gas lighting of Exeter's shop windows attracted favourable comments.

1816

500 pounds of beef and mutton were distributed to the poor of Alphington.

the Olden Time' thus alludes to the Exeter Mummers – quoting from a scarce work of 1737 – *England's Hero – St George for England.*

At Christmas Eve, or at least very lately, were fellows wont to go about from house to house in Exeter, a-mumming, one of whom, in a (borrowed) Holland shirt, most gorgeously be-ribboned, over his waistcoat, &c, flourishing a faulchion very valiantly, entertains the admiring spectators thus:

> Oh! Here comes I, St George, a man of courage bold,
> And with my spear I winn'd three crowns of gold,
> I slew the Dragon, and brought him to the slaughter,
> And by that very means I married Sabra, the beauteous King of Egypt's daughter.

The old 'Mummers' disguising seems now to be translated to the Fifth of November night, but our old 'Mummers' were satisfied with their own rendering of the costume of the renowned individuals they attempted to resuscitate. Our modern Fifth of November gallants are more pronounced, and give us, in tinsel and cardboard, brilliant representations of the Knights of old, or the proud Turk in his gorgeous finery.

The country 'Mummers' had their code of law – anything verging upon intoxication was punished by a fine. A Turkey fig was used to keep the voice in order, and after a week or ten days' 'outing' the performers would share £3 or £4 each.

'The Waits' or 'Singers' on Christmas morning were almost universal in Exeter parishes, sixty years ago! Nor are they quite fossilised now, as during a wakeful, still Christmas night, we catch that pleasant echo of old memories and bygone days!

> 'Awake, awake, it is the happy morn'

Or,

> 'Hark, the herald angels sing,
> Glory to the new-born king.'

Accompanied as of old with violin, bass and flute. The musical portion was concluded with the cheerful 'Good night, or good morning, Mr so and so – a Merry Christmas and Happy New Year' to be followed by a pecuniary appeal on Boxing Day. The late Mr David Gilbert, the Cornish antiquary, thus refers this pleasing custom, in a publication of his on Ancient Christmas Carols – 'Just before Christmas Day, I was awakened in London, at the dead of the night, by the playing of the waits. On the conclusion of their solemn tunes, one of the performers exclaimed aloud – 'God bless you, my masters and mistresses, a Merry Christmas to you and a Happy New Year.'

Another of the incidents of this time was the gathering of the night-stragglers and early risers, to listen to the famous 'One Hundredth Psalm' in the nave of the Cathedral. The singers were placed on the western side of the organ screen, and subsequently in the minstrels' gallery on the north side of the nave. This was a picturesque and impressive scene in the dim twilight of a winter's morning, illuminated by a few candles, the red glare from which strongly contrasted with the faint rays of returning daylight from the eastern windows. But there was a needs-be for discontinuing this service, and since the year 1858 it has ceased to be one of the specialities of Exeter Cathedral. Some from among 'the night-stragglers and early risers' on emerging from the Cathedral, after the singing, would find their way across the yard towards St Martin's Church, outside whose porch 'curds and whey' were sold – a harmless, warming and acceptable beverage on a winter's morning.[18]

1817

A swindler, who travelled under the name of Hore and was described as being 'of a dark complexion, near the age of thirty, chubby-faced, and weak in one eye, wears a blue coat, buff breeches and boots', recently left Stoke Canon owing money to the landlord of the public house.

1818

Dense fog throughout Devon.

1819

The Duke and Duchess of Kent spent Christmas in Sidmouth.

1830s Christmas in the 'Good Old Times' at Kingsbridge

In 1876 a writer for *The Western Times* looked back upon earlier Christmases and castigated older people for presenting the past, and especially the manner in which Christmas was celebrated, as being superior to the then present time. He argued that the economic and social conditions of ordinary people had greatly improved and that, in relation to Christmas, most men and women had been reliant upon the charity of the rich to provide them with extra food to celebrate the holiday. Moreover, he considered the ritual of begging to be demeaning. He contrasted this with the current situation where working men and women were able to provide for themselves.

Christmas is come, children have returned to their parental homes, relations are visiting, and friends have spent a day or two with old acquaintances. As usual, feasting is freely indulged in, in fact it would not otherwise be like Christmas. The season in this locality is being kept in a becoming manner, very different from what it was forty or fifty years since. Those not old enough to remember the 'good old times' will scarcely believe that such a revolution in manners and customs could have taken place in so short a time. Previous to the year 1832, and some years after, there was a vast amount of poverty in this district, farm labourers earned 7s a week, and mechanics from 10s to 12s. The farm labourer was little better than a serf. The village tradesman could scarcely venture to call his soul his own in the presence of his betters, and the small farmer did not venture an opinion in opposition to the squire and parson. But in addition to low wages there was another difficulty to contend with – the high price of provisions, the Tory government having taxed everything eaten, drunk or worn by the public. The consequence was difficulty for those in the lower grades of society to obtain the commonest food at regular times, therefore having something extra at Christmas by their own exertions was out of the question.

Everything bore the stamp of poverty; the cottages were of the meanest description, and the education of the children was nil in these 'good old times' when men, and women too, were daily taught to reverence their superiors, which of course meant their Squire and his family, and ditto the Parson. Then also there was a great deal of the feudal system in practice the great men of the parish and the more opulent farmers or small landowners would invite the commonality to their houses on Christmas Day, when there was a plain but liberal feast provided, and for this Christmas treat the recipient in return rendered obedience to his betters until

Christmas came round again. At that time there was a practice among a certain class of going about begging the day before Christmas. The women would dress themselves in their meanest clothes and perambulate the parish calling at every farmhouse where they were likely to obtain 'something for Christmas' At one place they would receive a pint of corn, and at another a quart, and frequently meat and drink. In this town for many hours in the early part of the day, groups of women and children, and sometimes infirm men, perambulated the streets – what was then termed 'mumping'. At certain drapers' shops they would receive a ball of cotton or some other trifle; at the candle maker's ship a halfpenny candle; gentlemen of independent means would give an applicant a penny, and in two or three cases the more affluent would give 2d to every beggar. Such was the poverty, such the high prices of the taxed articles, such the moral ignorance, and such the slavery of body and mind, that to obtain a few extra pence at Christmas women could so lower themselves that they were not ashamed to dress in the meanest manner and creep, cringe and demean themselves for such a contemptive charity. Such was the state of this neighbourhood only a few years ago, but an extraordinary change has taken place since then: a more enlightened class of statesmen has been called upon to govern the nation, the taxes have been removed from the necessaries of life, wages have gone up, education has made rapid strides, the cheap Press has put a newspaper into the hands of every man, and the consequence of all this is that the people had never better homes, better teaching, and as a natural result everyone can have a treat at his own house at his own expense. The working man, by reading the papers and the various publications of the day, has become a thinking man, and being a thinker, he has thrown off his 'feudal serfdom' and whilst he would still treat his 'betters' with becoming respect, he scorns to become their serf or your 'humble servant'. There are some people forever talking of the good old times and sorely lamenting the present state of things. Of course they do – they feel their power is gone; it is true there are many even now who will accept a 'gratis dinner' but the thinking part of even the working classes prefer a dinner of their own earning with independence to a sumptuous repast given in the shape even of patronage, leave alone charity. This much is certain, that Christmas is kept in a very different way from what it was forty years ago, and none but a madman would say that the manner of keeping Christmas in 1876 is not the most preferable.[19]

The argument for Christmas in 1876 being better than before is also made by a newspaper report entitled 'Old English Hospitality' which appeared on 31 December 1831 in *Woolmer's Gazette*.

On Thursday, the 22nd instant, Edward Drewe, Esquire of the Grange, in this county, had two fine bullocks slaughtered and distributed in suitable portions, according to the size of their families, among the poor of the parish of Broadhembury, thereby gladdening the hearts of the cottagers, by enabling them to partake in their humble homes, at this festive season, of that good old substantial fare, for the love of which John Bull is proverbial. This is the third time this kind-hearted and liberal gentleman has regaled the poor of his neighbourhood, since his return to his seat, a short period of only – months. Nor is this a solitary instance in our favoured county. John Gubbin Newton esquire of Millaton House, Bridestowe, last week distributed among his labourers and cottage tenants, a fine fat ox and seven sheep, together with suitable quantities of vegetables and food for firing. Mr N. Also on Christmas Day provided at his own house, a bountiful and substantial supper, with strong beer and grog for the church choir of Bridestowe, towards the proper support and keeping up of which, he is a most liberal annual benefactor. The Right Hon. Lord Rolle also caused to be distributed several fine oxen; indeed there are but a few of our nobility, and wealthy landowners who did not display similar acts of philanthropy, to their dependents and poorer neighbours. We cannot help thinking, that were these praiseworthy examples of hospitality towards the agricultural poor, more general in some other counties, we should not have to hear so often of the horrible acts of the incendiary, from which our county is at present happily free. Through the hardships of the times, or it may be some other cause, the poor are estranged from their superiors, and this link of society, seems in some places, almost riven asunder. It remains for the wealthy to step forward as in olden time, and by acts of true benevolence and kindness to heal the breach, and conciliate the oppressed poor, by letting them feel that they really care for their welfare.[20]

1820

A circus performed at Plymouth through Christmas Week.

1821

On Christmas morning an elderly man, who was accompanying a group of carol singers, fell into the river Exe near Exeter and drowned.

1822

A Totnes gooseberry bush was in full bloom through Christmas.

1823

The mutton, veal and lamb on show in the Exeter butcher's market attracted favourable comment as did the amount of turkeys, geese, fowls and woodcocks on show in St Martin's lane prompting the editor to write 'that want was a stranger to our city'.

1824
Exeter's Broadgate stood for its last Christmas; a few days later it was pulled down.

1825
The prisoners in Exeter's gaol were given a dinner of beef with plum pudding.

1826
Choirs sang Christmas carols throughout Exeter.

1826
On December 26th the cornerstone of Exeter's new marketplace was laid and the workmen were 'regaled with a proper quantum of strong beer'.

1827
Two days after Christmas firewood was distributed among the poor of Bicton.

1830s Plymouth customs

In 1882 a writer identified only by the initials 'J.E.' recorded his memories of Christmas in the 1830s.

In Plymouth, fifty years ago, a few days before Christmas, schoolmasters, their assistants, and scholars, were all busily engaged preparing their Christmas plays, for the purpose of exhibiting to the parents, friends and relatives, the progress the pupils had made in their studies during the year. One schoolmaster kept a school in a court, at the back of a small fruit ship, where now stands Popham and Radford's (drapers) ship. Fifty years ago the place was called 'Pig Market' now it is Bedford Street. This schoolmaster would always do his best to make a grand thing of these Christmas exhibitions. He would engage the hall of the Old Mechanics' Institute, and there, on a temporary platform, decorated with laurel, holly, candles, flowers and gilded pumpkins, would the pupils recite the declaim in their various parts to an admiring audience of friends and relatives. At the opening of the play, a pupil comes to the front, and recites a 'Prologue' having reference to the school, to the audience, and to Merry Christmas; the next pupil comes on and recites before the audience 'Pity the sorrows of a poor old man'. Another pupil recites the 'Three Black Crows', a fourth would declaim on Norval &c. This task over then follows the tea and cakes and fruit, and last of all, the sprightly dance. Other schools, fifty years ago, would at Christmas adopt a different scheme; the schoolmaster would give rewards and presents to those pupils who had best attended the school, and to those who had made the greatest progress in their learning. In some cases books were given to the public, to others would be presented a Christmas piece, which was a sheet of paper, about 20 inches long, by 15 inches wide. At the top part was printed in colours a picture of the Nativity, or Moses striking the rock; on the sides were a border illustrated with references to the top picture; in the centre of the sheet, a space of 12 inches by 10 inches was left blank for the purpose of inserting some appropriate scripture subject, to be done either in Text, Old English, or Engrossing and when it was well done it seemed to please every one who saw it. These Christmas pieces were exhibited in the booksellers' shop windows, and were just as numerous then as Christmas cards are now.[21]

1831 A Christmas gin shop

On Christmas Eve in 1831 Eliza Lovel of Exeter was accused of drunkenness and indecent behaviour and brought before the justices at Exeter's Guildhall. Because of her previous behaviour she was liable to 3 months' imprisonment but the justice 'with his accustomed clemency, sent her to spend [only] the Christmas Week in prison, seriously to reflect upon her folly and wickedness'. She may have benefited by reading the following lines on Exeter's gin shops which appeared in the local newspaper only a few days later while she was still incarcerated.[22]

An Ode to a Gin Shop (dedicated to the Tipple-ologers of Exeter)

'Oh that men should put an enemy in their mouths, to steal away their brains!'

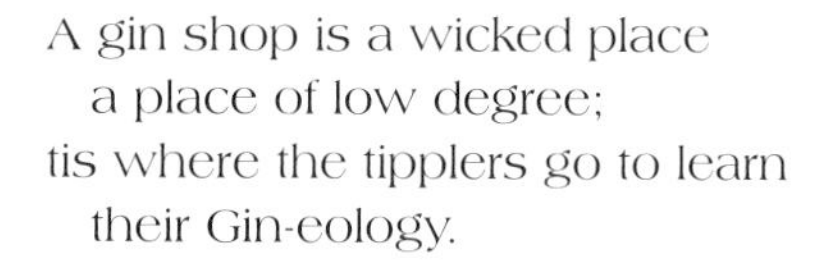
A gin shop is a wicked place
  a place of low degree;
tis where the tipplers go to learn
  their Gin-eology.

It is a place of much resort,
  where molly has her Will
The sailor goes to meet his lass,
  and Joan goes for her Gill.

Burning spirits here prevail,
  Black ruin and disgrace
Blue ruin's on the other side,
  And stares you in the face.

This is a place infected much,
  And here disease will taint,
For those who take their drops will catch,
  A Drop-sical complaint.

The men, likewise, are foppish here,
  And proud as any lass,
For like the women, they are fond
  of looking in their glass.

The liquor and tobacco here,
  So sweetly will perfume
The breath with odours, and twill give
  The nose a brandy bloom.

The tapster here declares, that he
  with honesty abounds
And yet he gives it out in drams,
  And takes it in by pounds.

There's some will tipple from a bowl,
  And then the lemon munch,
And make their stomachs puppet shows,
  Because they swallow punch.

To see these men all reeling home,
  Whenever such I know,
I go to view the funny sight,
  They make a pretty show.

Perhaps one will say he cannot stand,
  And then falls on his face,
So strangely speaking out the truth–
  Then lie with such a grace.

Ye drunkards all a warning take,
  And make no more delays,
But like my friend Mac'Adams,
  you should go and mend your ways.

But if you won't be thus advised,
  I vow again from me,
You shall another lecture have
  on Tipple-ology.

1828
Raspberry, strawberry and French beans were in flower in gardens throughout Devon.

1828
On Christmas Eve the rector of St Edmund's parish in Exeter gave a dinner, including roast beef, plum pudding, a pint of ale and a penny loaf, at the Anchor Inn for 31 of the eldest and poorest inhabitants.

1833 A Christmas play: *The Dying Miller* of Tavistock

In 1833 Anna Eliza Bray, novelist and a formidable writer on Dartmoor,[23] noted in a letter to Robert Southey a custom in Tavistock for which nothing else is known. She wrote:

Till within the last thirty years, the boys of this town, so I am informed, used every Christmas to act a standing old play, handed down by tradition, called *The Dying Miller*. Father Christmas was one of the characters, the New Year another, and Saint George performed sundry feats of valour. Mary Colling has very kindly exerted herself to try if she could recover for me any of the traditional doggerel assigned to the parts in this piece; some few lines she could remember having heard when a child. But hitherto we have not succeeded; though many of the elders remember the characters, and the style in which they dressed them.[24]

1836 The ashen faggot in Torquay

In 1873 William Pengelly, born a Cornishman but also, strangely, the 'father' of the Devonshire Association, reminisced about Christmas in Torquay.

I was present on Christmas Eve, 1836, in the old Torwood Manor House, Torquay, then occupied as a farmhouse by the late Mr John Mudge, when the 'ashen faggot' was prepared and burnt. It was 'made' in the farmyard, and bound together with as many 'binds' of withies as could be well put on it. When ready, it was as orthodoxy required, drawn to the front door of the house by four oxen, though a single ox would have been fully sufficient for greater labour, and taken thence and placed on the blazing hearth. Cards and other amusements occupied the juniors of the very large party, whilst the seniors, 'fast by the ingle bleezing finely' talked of 'old times'. All, however, were attentive to the fate of the 'binds' and as each *was observed* to 'give way' a demand for a gallon of cider was made on the farmer, who promptly supplied it.

The consumption of cider was certainly large, but so was the party; and no one seemed the worse for his or her potations.

At that time the custom was observed in all the principal farmhouses of the district, but it appears to be now a thing of the past.

1839 The landslip at Axmouth on Christmas morning

Late at night on Christmas Eve a number of labourers were returning to their cottages along the cliffs near Axmouth. They had spent the night at Dowlands Farm, the home of Mr Chappel, their employer, and enjoyed his hospitality: the ashen faggot had been burning in the hearth and presumably they had eaten a traditional meal of beef and ale. As the workers arrived at their homes they noticed that an existing subsidence had moved a further foot since they had left home that morning.

Events took a dramatic turn a few hours later: they were all disturbed from their sleep at about four in the morning by the walls of their homes rending and sinking, and seeing a fissure open in the ground before them. Shortly afterwards, on Christmas Morning, they returned to Dowlands and found that their way was nearly obscured by further earth movements. They discovered at the farm that buildings there too were ruined and as the day passed new fissures opened on the undercliff. A great chasm opened Christmas Night and within a short time it measured ¾ of a mile long, 150 feet deep and 300 feet wide. It was estimated that some 8,000,000 tons of earth collapsed.

Several coastguardmen were on duty Christmas Night and saw flashing lights and experienced an 'intolerable stench'. They also witnessed the sea appearing to be in agitation as the beach rose and fell, and the land along the coast gained in height. On Boxing Day the chasm continued to sink while the elevated reef rose still further.

The events of Christmas Eve, Christmas and Boxing Day attracted crowds of locals who came to wonder at the earth movements as they still do today.[25]

1829

Largesse was distributed at Bicton: clothing, firewood, beef and strong beer were given to the poor, on Christmas morning a breakfast consisting of strong beer, toasted cakes and sugar, was provided to the 'aged men servants', on the following day all the labourers were given a supper of roast beef and plum pudding and then afterwards all the household servants were given a Ball.

1830
Hedge strawberries were gathered on Christmas morning at Buckeridge Farm, the firemen of the West of England Office attended the Cathedral service in their new uniforms and the river Exe was frozen at Exeter.

1831
On Christmas evening fire destroyed 200 bags of potatoes & 100 bushels of oats in an Alphington storehouse

1840 Christmas gifts from Castle Hill to the poor of Challacombe

The Fortescue family of Castle Hill near South Molton regularly gave items of clothing to local poor families. In 1840 they provided 14 shifts, 13 shirts, 6 petticoats and 7 caps for poor men and women who lived in the parish Challacombe near Exmoor.[26]

	shift	shirt	petticoat	cap
Fry, John and wife	1	1		
Harris, John and wife	1	1		
Harris, Mary	1	1		
Jones, John and wife	1	1		
Lanceys, Margaret	1	1	1	
Laramy, Mary	1	1	1	
Nicholls, Joseph and wife	1	1		
Parkin, William and wife	1	1	1	
Pile, Mary	1	1	1	
Ridd, Ambrose and wife	1			
Ridd, Elizabeth	1	1	1	
Ridd, William and wife	1	1	1	1
Ash, George	1	1		
Downe, John	1	1		
Parkin, John	1	1		
Ridd, Ambrose	1	1		
Totterdale, James	1			
Wilkey, Richard	1			
Total	14	13	6	7

1841 Christmas hedges at Burlescombe

Three days before Christmas in 1841 a hedge-making competition took place in Burlescombe near Tiverton. It was reported in *Woolmer's Exeter and Plymouth Gazette*.

On Wednesday 22nd, a very interesting exhibition took place at Burlescombe, in this county. Several of the respectable inhabitants had subscribed to purchase shovels, two-bills, hooks &c as prizes for the most expert hedgers. The candidates were assembled in a meadow belonging to Mr Morgan: twenty feet of the hedge were measured off for each, who were required to sink the ditches, cast up the bank, fill up the middle, layer the quick, and make the wood into faggots under one bind, and the browse into nickeys, which means provincially very small faggots.

These nickeys are recommended as very convenient and safe for the farm oven and kitchen hearth. The men did the work cleverly in three hours, the time allowed, although much impeded by the wet and melted snow. Afterwards the party dined together and the usual toasts on such occasions were given. The umpires (who were respectable and practical yeomen from three parishes in the neighbourhood) now produced their award, and the prizes were distributed among the men. The umpires represented that the hedging was of a superior kind, but that the men might improve in making up the wood.

The poor fellows were then regaled with good Old Christmas fare and were as happy as their masters. The evening passed away with the best good humour. The men hoped for another such a spree and the masters were determined to gratify them again next year.[27]

1832

The prisoners of Devon County Gaol had a meal of one pound of mutton and a pint of beer each.

1833

At Castle Hill in Filleigh Countess Fortescue provided clothing for 200 poor people.

1842 Christmas under foot in Exeter

According to one press report, Christmas in Exeter in 1842 was not very pleasant owing to the 'scavengers', the street cleaners, having time off from work (like everyone else).

On Monday, being the day appointed for a general holiday in this city, in consideration of Christmas falling on a Sunday, the shops and warehouses were very generally closed, and the opportunity availed of by those engaged in them to suspend business and enjoy themselves. It was remarked that among the lower orders of labourers, the observance of the holiday was carried out with rigour, the cessation of the scavengers being particularly obvious, in the soiled shoes of those who would have preferred an unexceptional standing in Society.[28]

1846 An abstemious and Brazilian Christmas at Plymouth

Two separate observances of Christmas were reported by *The Plymouth and Devonport Weekly* on 31 December 1846.

The Plymouth Temperance Society held their annual Christmas festival at the Mechanics Institute, Princess Square, on Monday last, and although another party

1835
On the evening of December 22 a firework display took place over Southernhay, Exeter.

1836
On Christmas Eve a parishioner of St Edmund's publicly questioned whether the minister's sermons were worth hearing at half a penny each.

took place the same day, upwards of 200 persons were present. W. Bryant, Esquire, took the Chair. After tea, the Reverends Messrs Micklewood, Curtis and Clarke, and Mr Edmund Fry delivered very instructive addresses against intemperance, pointing out the benefits resulting from the adoption of Total Abstinence. The Secretary and Treasurer then gave in their reports, which were encouraging, and gave great satisfaction to all present. A vote of thanks was proposed to Mr Bryant, for his able conduct in the chair, as also to the musicians, both vocal and instrumental, for their kind assistance, and the meeting separated highly gratified with the proceedings of the evening. The appearance of the members was very gratifying. They are, generally, very healthy looking in their appearance, and their countenances would furnish a good character for the excellence of their principles.

Stonehouse Catholic Chapel – this chapel was crowded on Christmas Day by a very respectable audience who attended to witness the performance of High Mass. The chaplain attached to the Brazilian Frigate was the officiating High Priest, and he was assisted by the Rev. Mr Riley and the Rev. Mr O'Caroll in the performance of the imposing ceremonies. The Brazilian chaplain has a fine deep toned voice, which sounded exceedingly well in his chanting of the services. The Rev. Mr Bampton will shortly take the vows as a Jesuit, having only lately returned from Stonyhurst, where he has been studying for several years. The Brazilian band occupied one side of the gallery and played three or four times. Most of the Brazilian officers were present, and occupied a position immediately in front of the altar. The services lasted altogether nearly three hours.[29]

1847 Intolerance at Plymouth

The prejudice against Catholics was an issue raised by *The Plymouth and Devonport Weekly Journal* in 1847. It complements the report given in the previous year.

We are on the Hoe. The men of war seem to have retired out of respect for the day. A strong squadron of vessels consecrated to commerce and the arts of peace occupy the Sound. One would think all the merchant seamen had agreed to spend Christmas Day in the port of Plymouth. Not a soul is there on the Hoe save half a dozen very pretty children in warm scarlet Christmas-looking cloaks of the age Byron contemplates when he sings 'Sweet is the lisp of children and their earliest words'. Here are tempting subjects suggested by a stroll – peace, commerce, childhood, it would be dangerous to pause – let us quit the Hoe.

If there be one influence more pure and acceptable than another of the many which spring up at this season of the year, it is that of the almost universal feeling of charity (we do not mean mere alms-giving but a Christian recognition of all opinions).

Christmas revives the habitual charity that sleepeth. It creates the plant where yet it grew not. At Christmas even the most hopeless and ascetic bigots assume a virtue, and hang out the flag and sign of charity. In returning from the Hoe we observed some miserable ragged Irish going to the Catholic chapel. Now no one on such a day could find it in his heart to stigmatise these poor creatures as *idolaters*. They, if any, were surely sincere, they were ill-fed and scantily clothed, there was no parade of gilt-edged prayer book, or displaying of Sunday finery – they were 'publicans' and not 'pharisees'. Nothing so deeply pains us as the too frequent sweeping denunciations of Catholics as idolaters by many pious and sincere Protestants. It is very possible, it is truly said, to entertain both a foolish and superstitious hatred of even superstition and folly. 'Judge not that ye be not judged'. 'Let every man be fully persuaded in his own mind'.[30]

1838

More than twenty French vessels arrived at Plymouth with cargoes of grain.

1839

Mild weather continued and in Berrynarbor wild flowers were picked including cranesbill, dandelion, strawberry, groundsel, fumitory, blackberry, feverfew, white nettle, periwinkle, daisy, primrose, thistle, hemlock, veronica and violets.

1849 Victorian advice on Christmas

An editorial in *Trewman's Exeter Flying Post* suggested how its readers should observe the holidays.

Keep all those old seasonal observances which time has hallowed, which create good feeling and fellowship, and consist of those innocent recreations in which the young join as actors and which the old enjoy as spectators.

Be sure and decorate your house with holly. Evergreens are Nature's promise of returning summer and a fruitful season. The scarlet berries are pretty and cheerful, and the prickly leaves are excellent weapons to disperse the 'blue devils' which, with proper management, will become extinct at Christmas time.

Make up your mind to do some little good every day. Farthings make pence, pence shillings, shillings pounds, and pounds a rich man. Small charities, in like manner, soon mount up, and with care a good capital of happiness may be realised.

Pay off every debt of kindness that you are able, and call in, by gentle remembrances, all that are owing to you.

Be not content with giving your blankets and your coals to the poor: warm their hearts with kind language, as their bodies with good clothing.

Establish a court of equity in your heart, wherein to pronounce sentence on any of those domestic errors and crimes of which the law can take no cognisance. Make your good sense the judge, and the wholesome commandments of Scripture your jury. Examine and cross examine the witnesses: listen to the council for the plaintiff (Mr Feeling) and the counsel for the defendant (Mr Passion). You already know the evidence, and if the jury return a verdict of guilty, lay a heavy fine on the delinquent, and bind him in heavy sureties to keep in future the moral peace which he has violated.

1841
Six silver spoons, a cruet stand, and a small box were stolen from a cottage in Alphington.

1842
On Christmas Eve nine houses in Ottery St Mary were destroyed by fire.

1843
A wild strawberry was picked at Stoke Hill near Exeter.

1850 Christmas Eve in Devonshire

F. Stockdale, the writer and artist, wrote the following account of Christmas in Devon in *The Illustrated London News*.

Christmas is a season when the heart of man is evidently enlarged by sympathies of hospitality towards his fellow-creatures, in providing good cheer for himself and those whom Fortune has less favoured. Nowhere is this more substantially realised than amongst the farmers of Devon, who also preserve forms and ceremonies which the march of intellect has swept from other places. Ourselves wishing to see some of the sports in which our forefathers revelled, stepped over on Christmas Eve to Farmer B's. Passing the village, we were surprised at the silence prevailing; but an old woman cleared the mystery, by saying, 'all the volk be up at the varm' and approaching this, the loud laugh and cheering light streaming through the chequered glass – making more dark the dull cold night without – told of a warm reception within. Entering the kitchen amidst steam reeking from huge rounds of beef, joints of pork, heaps of turnips and potatoes, with puddings of monster rotundity, we discovered the burly host dealing out with unsparing hand to gladden the hearts of his lusty labourers. And truly, each seemed possessed of an appetite equal to the occasion – and, we trust, with powers of digestion such as we dyspeptics know of but by hearsay. Cider also flowed abundantly; and we felt that this meal to the man who receives but 6s or 7s a week as wages, must have proved a feast on which he could dwell with a satisfying delight. We could not but consider that the scene before us disproved the landlords' assertion so frequently made, and responded to by the gallant yeoman, 'that the farmers are in a starving condition' nor could we see that our host's provisions enjoyed protection, for all seemed to make free-trade with them.

'Bring in the faggot!'
'Behold him here!'

Faggots like most things, are by many in these parts termed of the masculine distinction.

'Clear the way!'

Now the ashen mass of 3 cwt, is raised on the [fire]dogs of the hearth, and in a few minutes the blaze from the scissing, crackling sticks, heightened the ruddy hue of the rustic guests. Song succeeded song, and when one presented more stupidity than another, shouts of laughter and bravos applauded to the skies. Now and then a fine voice broke upon the ear, leading us to regret that it was possessed by those whose souls had never been attuned to harmony. Many of their tunes were of the old English ballad class, and charmed us, not only as beings of the past, but having beauty in melody. Our hostess singing the song of 'Barbara Allen' awakened the memory of emotions of the past; for we had listened to this song on a similar festivity, now thirty years agone. Thou rapid, rolling flood – O time! Where hast thou borne those lips that sang, those ears that listened, those hearts that warmed with ours, leaving us alone to live again the associate scene?

Hark! What shout is that on which confusion seizes all – men, women and children, rushing pell-mell, scrambling to the highest bench – 'The mummers are coming, hurrah! The mummers are coming, hurrah!' And then entered six or seven youths fantastically bedecked with ribbons and gay, antiquated garments, ransacked from the bureaus of the grand-dames; here and there, a new bright silken bow, worn as a favour from their own dear Marys. Space being cleared, the play representing the unconquerable of old England partially attracted the attention of the noisy audience. A warrior, lip corked *a la moustache*, personating the ambitious Napoleon, is brought to encounter St George, who after a fierce encounter, lays the vaunting Gallic dead upon the earth, the wall echoing the boisterous applause that greets his downfall. However, by the interposition of old Father Christmas, he is restored to partake again of the season's blessings.

Near this point our Sketch is taken. At the right are seated those whose hunger craves relief, which the farmer's wife is labouring to accord. Facing are they who, with their senses quickened by the juice of apple, shout at the valiant heroes. Inclining against the chimney, behold the farmer watching to supply the wants of any of his friends. Beneath are placed a group of children, whose minds are wondering at so strange a sight. The old sheep-dog, from custom, appears a complacent observer; whilst the younger one barks at the quaint intruders. Above the door the fiddlers three add discord to the din; and from confusion worse confounded we gladly made a retreat.[33]

1844

A 'group of nature's eccentricies' were exhibited at Exeter through the Christmas season including a man who weighed 600 pounds and had six toes on each foot.

I YIELD TO THE PRESSURE FROM WITHOUT.

c.1850 Recipes for Christmas Pudding and Yuletide Cake from Drewsteignton

These two recipes were recorded in a manuscript book which belonged to John Grendon of Drewsteignton and appear to have been written in the middle of the nineteenth century.

Christmas Pudding

1 lb of raisins, 1 lb of currants, 1 lb beef suet, ¼ lb moist sugar, ½ lb flour, 1 lb bread crumbs, 4 eggs, ¼ lb citron, ¼ lb candied lemon peel, half pint new milk, one gill of rum, brandy or whiskey, mixed altogether. A rich plum pudding of this kind cannot be boiled too long; the longer it is boiled the more wholesome it is.

GET INTO HOT WATER.

Yule Tide Cake

Place 1 lb of fresh butter in a pan, keep it near the fire till melted. Stir into it 1 lb of powdered loaf sugar, a good tablespoonful each of beaten allspice and cinnamon by degrees put in the yolks of ten eggs and their whites separately whisked to a froth, add 1 lb of candied citron sliced thin, 2 lbs of currants cleaned and dried, 2 oz of blanched sweet almonds, 1 ½ lbs of flour and a gill of brandy. Mix all well together and bake it for four hours in a slow oven.[32]

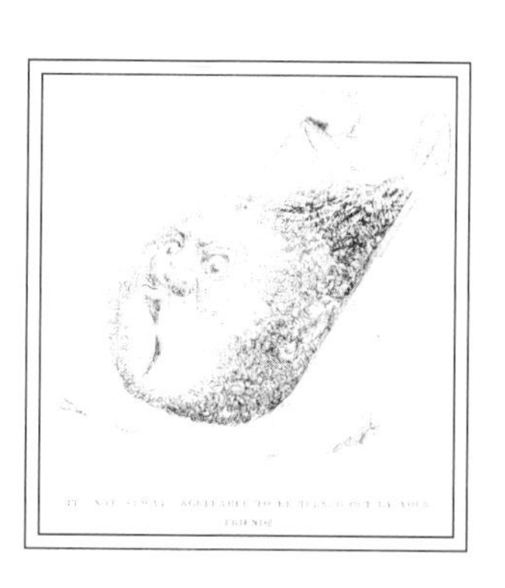

I MAKE MY DEBUT.

AM CUT UP, THOUGH NOT BY THE CRITICS.

I AM NOT UNIVERSALLY POPULAR.

THE VAIN FEELINGS OF MY YOUTH PASS AWAY;

1850 and 1851 The Sidmouth mummers and Peter Orlando Hutchinson

For several years in the middle of the nineteenth century Peter Orlando Hutchinson, the premier diarist and writer of Sidmouth, recorded his impressions of the local mummers. In 1848 he had noted that on Christmas Day 'The mummers muster [was] strong this year. Some parties dressed in the uniforms of naval officers and some as officers of the army. One personage in Turkish costume generally accompanying them...' His diary entries for 1850 and 1851 are very informative but present a great contrast with another local who later wrote in 1865.

1850 Christmas Eve

All day today the town was in a din with sundry noises. The church bells were continually ringing and the mummers were blowing their horn, first down one road, then up another. As usual, they composed a company of five or six boys, one being in a Turkish or some Eastern costume, and the rest for the most part in blue naval uniforms. This, however, is not constant, and of course the dresses will vary, so as to suit the drama enacted. The great naval hero personified is Lord Nelson, and when the piece is of a military character, the Duke of Wellington plays the chief part. I know not what dramas the ancient mummers players, but the wars of Napoleon Bonaparte's time furnish incidents for almost all the performances of our modern mummers at Sidmouth. As soon as it was dark out came the carol singers, mostly little girls of ten or twelve years old. Now and then we have a set of young men and women who sing in part, which is certainly more euphorious to the ear, for the children generally sing all in unison, which is very grating. The ancient carols were, of course, always of a religious nature, but this evening I heard some that did not seem to be so, either in words or tune. Later in the evening or rather throughout the night, the church singers went round. In times gone by we used to regale them with hot spiced drink when they came to our house in Coburg Terrace, but of late we have somehow omitted this. We did not omit this evening to burn the ashen faggot, but alas for its size! One might have put it into one's pocket.

1851 Christmas Day

A mild day like October and very fine with the exception of a shower or two. This evening I took a turn on the promenade on the beach. The quietness of the night was agreeably broken by the distant sounds of several parties of carol singers. One party up towards Witheby was very melodious, and seemed to have horns and opluclides with them. Another party, near Denby Row or Place, which afterwards came to Coburg Terrace, and which I enriched with two pence, sang very nicely in part, first, second, &c, though they were but young girls. The tunes were of a hymn-like character, and the words appropriate to the season. But the old tune, which I can remember for twenty-five years nearly in Sidmouth, runs thus:

The new tunes are mostly sung by the children who have had some instruction at the Sunday Schools, but those who have not had this tutorage keep to the old one. I questioned a party of Mummers as to whom they personated? One said 'I am the Duke of Wellington' another, 'I am Tipoo' (and I suppose of Saringapatam) and then said another 'I am the Prince of Orange' and then came 'Old Father Christmas', a little smooth-face boy. A strange medley.[31]

1845

A bouquet of primroses was picked at Whitestone near Exeter.

1846

Bideford shops were closed on December 26th in order for the male workers to visit their friends.

1847

There were concerns in Heavitree about the safety of the Liverydole almshouses after the garden wall fell down.

1852 The wreck of the *Ocean Queen* at the Mew Stone

The weather over Christmas in 1852 was particularly miserable. A great storm roared up the English Channel and caused widespread damage throughout the country. Devon suffered particularly badly including a yacht and barge being sunk at Plymouth and 40 tons of coal washed away at Millbay Pier. The coast guard who was on duty at Yealm Station discovered pieces of the wreck of a large ship on Wembury Church beach. The name of the vessel was painted in white letters – the *Ocean Queen* of London, a ship which was estimated to be of 400 tons burthen. It was supposed that the master had been attempting to enter Plymouth harbour when the vessel became entangled on the reefs of the Great and Little Mew Stones. The body of a 30 year-old mariner washed ashore and all others of the 30 member crew were presumed drowned. It was also assumed that the vessel was destined for the West Indies and some of the cargo also washed ashore including unbleached calico, ladies dresses, women's straw bonnets and turnovers, thousands of reels of cotton thread, men's shirts and woollen Scottish caps.[34]

1852 Christmas in Exeter Cathedral

The Illustrated London News reported on Christmas in Exeter Cathedral in its special seasonal issue.

The custom of welcoming this season of holy joy with 'psalms and hymns and spiritual songs' lingers in the cathedral city of Exeter where, during Christmas Eve the parish choirs perambulate the streets singing anthems, with instrumental accompaniments. The singing is protracted through the night, when the celebration often assumes a more secular character than is strictly in accordance with the festival. A more sacred commemoration is, however, at hand.

At a quarter past seven o'clock on Christmas morning the assemblage of persons in the nave of Exeter Cathedral is usually very numerous: there are the remnants of the previous vigil, with unwashed faces and sleepy eyes; but a large number are early risers, who have left their beds for better purposes than a revel. There is a great muster of the choir, and the fine Old Hundredth Psalm is sung from the gallery to a full organ, whose billows of sound roll through the vaulted edifice. The scene is strikingly picturesque: all is dim and shadowy; the red light from the flaring candles falling upon up-turned faces, and here and there falling upon a piece of graven sculpture, whilst the grey light of day begins to stream through the antique windows, adding to the solemnity of the scene. As the last verse of the Psalm peals forth, the crowd begins to move, and the spacious cathedral is soon left to the more devout few who remain to attend the morning services in the Lady Chapel.[35]

1854 Cutting the Ashen Faggot

In December 1854 *The Illustrated London News* reported on Devon's ashen faggots. It noted that:

Our illustration represents Cutting the Ashen Faggot. The ash is said to be the only wood that will burn green, and it is the policy of the wood-cutters to lay on as many 'binds' upon the faggot as possible, as it is an old established custom that every 'bind' should represent a jug of cider, not that this is the limitation of quantity consumed on the occasion, only that this is part of the ceremonial.

A hot supper is usually provided, and the wives and children of the labourers and servants, together with the farmer and his family form a jocund party, and there is no end of good solid cheer and hearty entertainment, which lasts far into the Christmas morning.[36]

1856 'Christmas Bells' by Edward Capern of Bideford

Edward Capern was a rural postman who walked 13 miles on his daily round for which he received ten shillings and six pence per week. He also wrote poems and songs.

Ring out, ye merry bells! Welcome bright icicles!
Welcome old holly-crowned Christmas again!
Blithe as a child at play, keeping his holiday,
Welcome him in from the snow-peak and plain.

Up with the holly-bough, green from the winter's brow;
Lock up your ledgers and cares for a day;
Out to the forest go, gather the mistletoe,
Old and young, rich and poor, up and away.

Up with the holly-bough, ay, and the laurel now;
In with the yule-log, and brighten the hearth;
Quick! He is here again, come with his joyous train,
Laughter, and Music, and Friendship, and Mirth.

Up with the holly-boughs, high in each manor house
Garnish the antlers that hang in the hall;
Yes, and the 'neck' of corn with a gay wreath adorn
Rich as the bloom on the cottager's wall.

Wealth has its duties now, Christians, you will allow;
Think then, ye rich, whilst your tables are spread,
Think of those wretched ones, Poverty's stricken sons,
Weeping, whilst children are asking for bread.

Ring out, ye merry bells! Ring till your music swells
Out o'er the mountain and far on the main;
Ring till those cheerless ones catch up your merry tones,
Singing, 'Come, Christmas, again and again.'[37]

1848
Shapcott's Sax-horn band played in the streets of Exeter.

1849
After a period of sharp frosts, Christmas Day in Torrington was warm and sunny followed shortly afterwards by a severe snowstorm in which ten inches of snow fell.

1850
Fire struck the house of a Torquay coal-merchant.

1851
The Mayor entertained members of the Exeter Police Force with a 'substantial supper and accompaniments' at the Turk's Head. At Dawlish men had been bathing in the morning at Cow's Hole up to the 20th of December.

1857 Edmund Gosse and the destruction of his Christmas pudding at Torquay

Edmund Gosse, poet and a man of letters, spent several years of his childhood living in Torquay with his father Philip Henry Gosse, the noted marine zoologist. The elder Gosse was a Plymouth Brethren who suggested that fossils were hidden by God to test the faith of scientists and strongly disapproved of the celebration of Christmas. Edmund Gosse was eight years old in 1857 and later remembered of his father at Torquay that:

On the subject of all feasts of the Church he held views of an almost grotesque peculiarity. He looked upon each of them as nugatory and worthless, but the keeping of Christmas appeared to him by far the most hateful, and nothing less than an act of idolatry. 'The very word is Popish', he used to exclaim, 'Christ's Mass!' pursing up his lips with the gesture of one who tastes asafoetida by accident. Then he would adduce the antiquary of the so-called feast, adapted from horrible heathen rites, and itself a soiled relic of the abominable Yule-Tide. He would denounce the horrors of Christmas until it almost made me blush to look at a holly berry.

On Christmas Day of this year 1857 our villa saw a very unusual sight. My Father had given strictest charge whatsoever was to be made in our meals on that day; the dinner was to be neither more copious than usual nor less so. He was obeyed, but the servants, secretly rebellious, made a small plum pudding for themselves (I discovered afterwards, with pain, that Miss Marks received a slice of it in her boudoir). Early in the afternoon, the maids – of whom we were now advanced to keeping two – kindly remarked that 'the poor dear child ought to have a bit, anyhow', and wheedled me into the kitchen, where I ate a slice of plum-pudding. Shortly I began to feel that pain inside which in my frail state was inevitable, and my conscience smote me violently. At length I could bear my spiritual anguish no longer and bursting into my study I called out 'Oh Papa, Papa, I have eaten of the flesh offered to idols!' It took some time, between my sobs, to explain what had happened. Then my Father sternly said 'Where is the accursed thing?' I explained that as much as was

left of it was still on the kitchen table. He took me by the hand, and ran with me into the midst of the startled servants, seized what remained of the pudding, and with the plate in one hand and me still tight in the other, ran till we reached the dust-heap, when he flung the idolatrous confectionary on to the middle of the ashes, and then raked it deep down into the mass. The suddenness, the violence, the velocity of this extraordinary act made an impression on my memory which nothing will ever efface.[38]

1852

Floods struck Exeter on Christmas Eve. This was the last Christmas Newton Abbot celebrated before adopting London time.

1862 Sabine Baring-Gould's Christmas at Lew Trenchard

In 1881 the Reverend Baring-Gould, author and rector of Lew Trenchard from that year, reminisced about an earlier Christmas, when he was aged 28 years old. He wrote that he was:

Alone, except for my little brother, in Lew House. The rats are celebrating Noel. They had a frolic last night, kept high festival, had a wild hunt. They scoured along the passages, they scampered between floor and ceiling, they danced a hornpipe in the storeroom and rollicked up and down the stairs. They kept me awake. Presently I heard the distant strains of carol singers and the groaning of an accompanying bass-viol. I ascertained in the morning that the performers were the choir of the Meeting House. The Church, buried in sleep, did not sing to greet the Saviour's birth. The chapel choir itinerated all night till five o'clock in the morning. They visited every house in the parish except those of the parson and the squire, for the former were too orthodox to tolerate dissenting music, and the latter was absent from home. At their return they were all the worse for liquor. In church this morning there were twelve persons, of these nearly all were from the Rectory.[39]

1853
At Teignmouth a Christmas Tree, provided for 50 poor people, was covered with 'various kinds of useful articles' such as gloves, comforters and hose.

1854
There were no public amusements of any kind in Dartmouth on Christmas Day.

1855
Ten pounds was distributed among Brixham's poor fishermen and fishermen's widows.

1865 Outrage and Midnight Mass at Teignmouth

The Western Times expressed moral outrage at the observance of midnight mass at Teignmouth in 1865.

The parish church of East Teignmouth has gained an unenviable sort of notoriety for its hankering after the rites and ceremonies of papistry, and many of the parishioners have long withdrawn themselves from its influence and become attendants at the sister establishment of worship, – or at the dissenting places of worship – of which there are several in the town. The incumbent seems determined, however, that his hobby shall be ridden to the utmost, and whether it be that in his admiration for the popish ritual he forgets he is a clergyman of the Church of England, or that feeling a spirit of opposition raised against his innovations he is determined to crush it, certain it is that his vagaries begin to assume a shape and character which cause regret not unmixed with serious alarm, in the minds of all who call themselves Protestants. Hitherto, indeed, there had been nothing worse than the mongrel high church practices now become so common in many places, but the proceedings at St Michael's Church on Sunday evening last were of a character probably unparalleled in any protestant community since the beginning of the Reformation.

On Saturday last it was rumoured about that there would be a service held in the church at midnight on Sunday – somewhat after the fashion adopted in some dissenting places of worship on the eve of the new year; and a vast concourse accordingly assembled outside the church doors in anticipation of the novelty. The time, it will be remembered, was verging on midnight, and not a few of the would-be congregation were youths, of both sexes, who, in the absence of any thought as to the religious import of the matter, freely indulged in that species of 'chaff' and banter one so commonly hears at the doors of a theatre on a night of some extraordinary attraction. In fact there could be no better illustration of the scene than to conjure up such an occasion. When at length the doors were opened, a flare of light from a number of wax candles over the Communion table directed attention to that part of the church, which bore all the appearance of a Roman Catholic Chapel wanting only the altar to complete the picture. The incumbent had given orders that the congregation should be limited to the under part of the church, consequently the five or six hundred people who pressed in were much straitened for room even to stand, and it was some time before the surging mass could be settled down to allow the ceremonies to commence. A voluntary on the organ introduced the choristers, who, after singing a verse of a hymn behind the screen of the vestry, issued the way to the Communion Table, and there began the service. Curiosity and the novelty of the proceedings mastered every other feeling, while the good sense of the people maintained that decorum which the sanctity of the place and the occasion demanded; but it was very evident that the vast majority of the assembly considered that their religious feelings were being outraged, and the purity of the Protestant faith assailed, in their being made subservient to the whims and predilections of a coterie. The Communion service was read through, the responses being chanted by the choristers, and the whole accompanied by those genuflexions and other characteristics of popery, which only lacked the swinging about of the incense vessel to render the semblance perfect.

After these preliminaries, the Holy Sacrament was administered to a few devotees, the organ meanwhile playing one of those soft and ravishing symphonies which so much heighten the effect of solemn ceremonies, and which, among the ignorant catholic, help to elevate the administration of the 'elements' with the real presence of the Deity. The church being so crowded, it was difficult, if not impossible, for any but those in the immediate vicinity of the Communion-table to tell what was going forward; in fact many unfavourably placed for observation thought from the anxiety manifested by some of the more inquiring among their fellow spectators, that nothing less than the 'elevation of the host' was being performed, and soon the seats and cushions became vantage ground from which perchance, a better and more general view could be obtained of the proceedings. Their thoughts, however, were speedily called from Heaven to the sordid things of earth, and the clinking of money into the plates of the collectors showed that the 'main chance' was not altogether omitted in the calculations of the rev. parson, who inducted the gathering, and exhausted the entire offertory sentences while awaiting the issue of this part of the business. A prayer for the whole church militant closed the service, and the choristers, having again formed in procession, moved towards the vestry, the incumbent bringing up the rear, and holding in his hands the proceeds of the occasion.

The organ then thundered forth a voluntary, and the church was speedily cleared of its congregation, who had ushered in the Christmas morning of 1865 in a manner as unusual as it is un-English in the present day. What the ultimate effect of this proceeding maybe it is difficult to say. To those who had before held scruples regarding the method of public worship adopted at East Teignmouth church, it will afford a bitter satisfaction to find that these scruples were not altogether groundless; to others, who have clung to the hope that a more conciliatory spirit would at some time or another exhibit itself in the deportment of the incumbent towards his flock, the scene attempted to be described will cause consternation and dismay. For, however tolerant and liberal-minded they may be in dealing with their fellow Christians of every shade of belief, it is more than human to expect that they will suffer these bitter pills of popery to be forcibly thrust down their throats without an effort at resistance.[40]

1856
Two days before Christmas a steamer sank at Teignmouth.

1857
A cheddar cheese weighing 123 pounds was on show in Exeter.

1858
'The Forty Thieves' was Exeter's pantomime.

1859
Christmas Day was wet and foggy throughout Devon.

1860
Snow fell throughout Devon during Christmas Week.

1865 Game for Christmas at Ottery St Mary

In 1865 *The Tiverton Times* printed a report, entitled 'Game For Christmas', that four young boys had misspent their Christmas.

John Potter, Charles Selway, William Vigers and William Selway, four stout young blades, were charged with ferreting rabbits on lands belonging to Sir John Kennaway on Christmas Day. The first three names pleaded guilty, the last put himself on his defence. John Gosling, the gamekeeper on the property, was keeping Christmas *al fresco* by looking after the movements of his active neighbours. Came into the plantation about three o'clock and saw three lads ferreting. After watching a good bit, he saw Charles Selway, the younger, in the act of replacing the net against the hedge. Hearing some talk outside the hedge, he went round to get a view of the talkers, and there saw Vigors and two smaller boys looking at him. Also saw William Selway and the others in the cover. Called to them and told them to give up their nets (produced). The defendant was one of the party running away. Potter had nets; he threw them into the hedge, where witness found them the next day.

The Bench held it proved that Master W.S. was at this Christmas game, and the magistrates admonished the father of the lad, who wished to speak for him, that he had better check him than defend him, for if he began with ferrets and nets he would bye and by get on to gins, and then to guns with all their bad consequences. They were required to pay 10 shillings each, to include costs, the latter item was £1 3s 6d.

'That's very hard,' grumbled out some relations aloud.[41]

1865 Sidmouth mummers

In 1865 one resident of Sidmouth expressed in *The Western Times* great disapproval of the mummers. His views contrast greatly with those of Peter Orlando Hutchinson written some fifteen years previously.

The Mummer and Mumster Nuisance

At Christmas and New Year, on May Day and Guy Fawkes day, parties of idle boys and men, sometimes masked, go round to the various houses at night, intruding into the gardens and grounds, and new comers particularly, are alarmed after the children are fast asleep by a sudden and violent 'Remember! Remember!' or a loud discordant hymn or song, which makes Paterfamilias very angry and startles mamma and the babes. Surely the magistrates and police can do something to put a stop to this, which has become a chronic and intolerable nuisance. The stillness of night is sometimes varied and made hideous by a German Brass Band (oh! for Mr Babbage), and morning reveals damage by fire balls, broken shrubs, and other mischief, if black mail is not submitted to, in addition to the annoyance otherwise.[42]

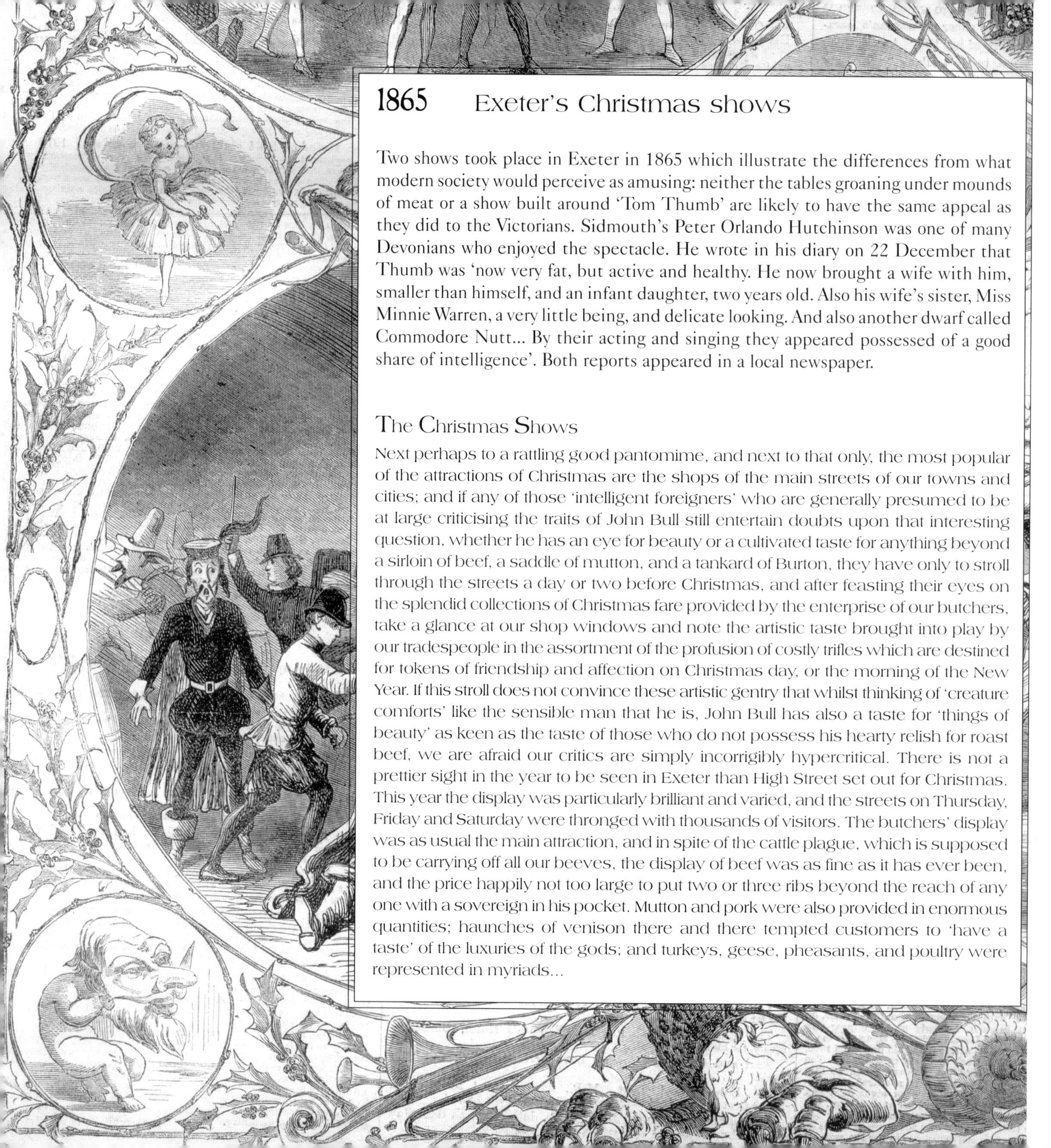

1865 Exeter's Christmas shows

Two shows took place in Exeter in 1865 which illustrate the differences from what modern society would perceive as amusing: neither the tables groaning under mounds of meat or a show built around 'Tom Thumb' are likely to have the same appeal as they did to the Victorians. Sidmouth's Peter Orlando Hutchinson was one of many Devonians who enjoyed the spectacle. He wrote in his diary on 22 December that Thumb was 'now very fat, but active and healthy. He now brought a wife with him, smaller than himself, and an infant daughter, two years old. Also his wife's sister, Miss Minnie Warren, a very little being, and delicate looking. And also another dwarf called Commodore Nutt... By their acting and singing they appeared possessed of a good share of intelligence'. Both reports appeared in a local newspaper.

The Christmas Shows

Next perhaps to a rattling good pantomime, and next to that only, the most popular of the attractions of Christmas are the shops of the main streets of our towns and cities; and if any of those 'intelligent foreigners' who are generally presumed to be at large criticising the traits of John Bull still entertain doubts upon that interesting question, whether he has an eye for beauty or a cultivated taste for anything beyond a sirloin of beef, a saddle of mutton, and a tankard of Burton, they have only to stroll through the streets a day or two before Christmas, and after feasting their eyes on the splendid collections of Christmas fare provided by the enterprise of our butchers, take a glance at our shop windows and note the artistic taste brought into play by our tradespeople in the assortment of the profusion of costly trifles which are destined for tokens of friendship and affection on Christmas day, or the morning of the New Year. If this stroll does not convince these artistic gentry that whilst thinking of 'creature comforts' like the sensible man that he is, John Bull has also a taste for 'things of beauty' as keen as the taste of those who do not possess his hearty relish for roast beef, we are afraid our critics are simply incorrigibly hypercritical. There is not a prettier sight in the year to be seen in Exeter than High Street set out for Christmas. This year the display was particularly brilliant and varied, and the streets on Thursday, Friday and Saturday were thronged with thousands of visitors. The butchers' display was as usual the main attraction, and in spite of the cattle plague, which is supposed to be carrying off all our beeves, the display of beef was as fine as it has ever been, and the price happily not too large to put two or three ribs beyond the reach of any one with a sovereign in his pocket. Mutton and pork were also provided in enormous quantities; haunches of venison there and there tempted customers to 'have a taste' of the luxuries of the gods; and turkeys, geese, pheasants, and poultry were represented in myriads...

General Tom Thumb and his wife are holding a series of levees at the Clarence Assembly Rooms. The first took place yesterday, and were in the morning and afternoon not only numerously but very fashionably attended, and in the evening the room was thronged. The party consists of the General, his wife and child, Commodore Nutt and Minnie Warren, the sister of the General's wife, and their entertainment, drawn up on the model of that of Mr and Mrs Howard Paul, is composed of songs, duets, and representations of 'character' – the General, for example, impersonating Napoleon Bonaparte. They go through their programme with surprising ease and liveliness, and keep the assembly in the best of humours throughout by their wit and repartee. This is the General's final tour through England, and he remains for the week. Apart from the entertainment itself, which is very diverting, this group of miniature humanity represents, we suppose, the smallest set of people in the world, possessing in their full vigour all the physical and mental powers of our race.[43]

1865 Christmas boxes at Exeter and King's Nympton

In 1865 the question of giving Christmas Boxes to workers was discussed in the pages of *The Exeter Flying Post*. Irrespective of this plaintive call made by 'Tiny Tim', a year later 25 tea dealers and grocers in Exeter discontinued the practice.[44]

Dear Sir

In one of your contemporaries 'A Resident in Exeter' calls upon the public to give double the usual fee as a Christmas Box; to the postman; very good indeed:

> Honour and shame from no condition rise,
> Act well your part, there all the honour lies.

There can be no possible objection to any person following 'A Resident in Exeter's dictum', should he feel so inclined, but I should imagine that few people will agree with his churlish remarks about us errand boys. Why should their ears be 'boxed'? 'A Resident in Exeter' should feel grateful for his own good fortune if he were never compelled to be 'a little errand boy'. Many of us small fellows work early and late, and much of the Christmas comforts of big people depend on our labours. Should not boys, small as well as big, be encouraged sometimes? We get plenty of boxes, such as he would distribute, all the year round, and a few we contrive to bestow on ourselves, but that is neither here nor there. We look forward to Christmas boxes very anxiously; some of us to purchase a useful garment, or make a present to a sister or mother, that the weekly wage is unequal to provide. Now, take us as a body, will this crabbed customer deny that we are a useful lot? Some of the most enterprising and successful men of the present day, we hear, started as errand boys. Therefore, don't rob Peter to pay Paul. Each is worthy of his hire – and his Christmas box. Remember the Postman – but don't cuff the 'Errand Boy'.

Tiny Tim

1861

Before Christmas, the table of Newton Poppleford's 'Knight of the Cleaver' on sale at Sidmouth collapsed under the weight of the meat.

1862

A lime-burner from Membury was accidentally killed in a gun accident.

An editor added '*Tiny Tim* is desirous that the *Flyer* should do him and those of his feather a good turn. We hope *Tiny Tim* is not one of those disgraceful young blackguards who smoke short pipes and talk filth up and down the High Street almost every evening, Sundays more especially, and to which 'A Resident in High Street' calls the attention of the authorities.'[45]

There was also a case made at King's Nympton for discontinuing boxes at Christmas.

A fight between 'Bob Brettle' and 'Jim Lightfoot' took place at the Carpenter's Arms on the shortest day of the waning year. As it was drawing near merry tide, perhaps they felt desirous of giving one another a Christmas 'box'. And so it proved to be, for Bob got ready, showing his science; Jim advanced and dealt him a good one on his left peeper; which brought Bob up to his antagonist in great fury. Jim was not the only sufferer by this scrimmage, for the essence of barley-corn was spilt all over the ground, and the table and Jim too were upset by Bob's fury. This concluded round the first. Round the second commenced with a little counter hitting, which closed by Bob receiving a stretcher on the floor. Round third – Both got ready and after a second or so of sparring. Brettle popped a good 'un into the right winker of Lightfoot, which made the claret run freely. The seconds could not prevail to get them to their corners for a second or so, but as true Englishmen, they were willing to fight in their blood, and prepared for another meeting, when a signal was given that the police had arrived. This ended the fight. It may well be supposed that they will neither of them enter the new year without their box, much to their disgrace, and to Brettle in particular, now arrived at the ripe age of there score and ten years. What a thing to behold and worse if all were told.[46]

1863
The parish church of Ashwater was decorated with strawberries.

1864
Early on Christmas morning a collision took place on the South Devon Railway at the Kingsbridge Road Station between a goods train and a passenger train delayed out of London by the great number of Christmas parcels and extra passengers.

1865 Disorderly at Christmas

Two individuals appeared before justices at Exeter Guildhall on 26 December accused of behaviour which has become as traditional as any over Christmas.

William Perriam was charged with creating a disturbance and assaulting P.C. Milford, in Guinea Street, on Christmas Eve. The officer, hearing a Babel of sounds in that quarter at 12.45, paid it a visit, when he found defendant actively abetting the confusion. Being requested to move on he refused, and repaid the caution given him with cuffs. He and others set upon the officer with such violence that they had likely to have made mince meat of him. The noise of the row brought Inspector Dunning to the rescue, when the cry of the rabble was give *et tu en; give et tu en*. Defendant was seized, and after much resistance, lodged in the lock up. Charles Wood, newsvendor, Milk Street, proved seeing defendant strike the policeman, and knock off his hat. As to the rows they occurred there almost every night of the week, so disorderly was it in that quarter. Defendant said that hearing singing he went in our of South Street to join, thinking they were regular singers, and there he was encountered by the officer – it was all his fault. The Bench were quite of opinion that he had been guilty of a very gross breach of the peace; and as police officers must be protected in the discharge of their duty, he was fined 20s and costs, or 14 days in prison.

Ann Williams was charged with being drunk and disorderly in the street, at about one o'clock in the morning. She was in Milk Street, driving her guilty trade, when first spoken to – one man who refused her solicitations she knocked over. She had the strength of a she-bear. Getting foul of a respectable man in Fore Street, she accused him of stealing her brooch and got herself taken care of by P.C. Full. Defendant said the officer put improper questions to her, and she answered them, accordingly. Being a recent importation from the Channel Islands, it was her first appearance before the Exeter Bench; she was, therefore, leniently fined 5 shillings only and costs, or a week.[47]

1866 Christmas in Bideford and Crediton

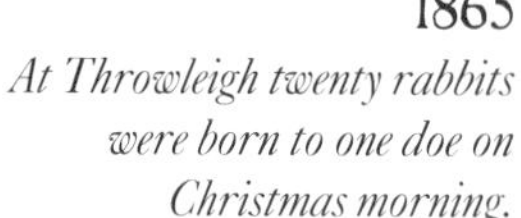
1865
At Throwleigh twenty rabbits were born to one doe on Christmas morning.

The Western Times reported noisy nights in two Devon towns on Christmas Eve.

Bideford

Some members of the band of the 26th Devon Rifles played several select pieces in different parts of the town about midnight on Christmas Eve. It was very pleasant to be awakened to hear such sweet strains. The singers made a different impression: the performance was bad, by whomsoever enacted. The days of good singing have passed in this town.

There were to be seen in the window of Mrs McNamara, Mill Street, Bideford, last week about a dozen pears, of the second gathering, from a tree belonging to Mr Thomas Bell, Abbotsham. Likewise a bunch of scented violets, gathered near this town.

The shops were all closed on Wednesday [December 26th], and had the weather been frosty the town would have had a real Christmas appearance. It was dirty under feet, although dry over head.

Crediton

As usual on Christmas Eve and the early hours of Christmas Day, sleep was transported from this town. Old customs are not to be dispensed with without a struggle, so the ash-faggots had to be burnt, and carols had to be sung – the number of the first would be a difficulty to get at, the list of the second would be a still greater difficulty. Whilst some employed their vocal powers in raving 'We won't go home till morning' the strains of the choirs of the Church of England, and Nonconformist congregations were marked by almost angelic strains. At early dawn the parish bells announced the Great Birthday. [48]

1868 'Christmas Day' by Charles Kingsley

The author Charles Kingsley, best known in regards to Devon for *Westward Ho!*, wrote 'Christmas Day'. He composed it shortly after his son left for South America.

How will it dawn, the coming Christmas Day?
  A Northern Christmas, such as painter love,
And kinsmen, shaking hands but once a year,
  And dames who tell old legends by the fire?
Red sky, blue sky, white snow and pearled ice,
  Keen ringing air, which sets the blood on fire,
And makes the old man merry with the young,
  Through the short sunshine, through the longer night?

1866
A wild strawberry was picked on Christmas day in Black Torrington.

Or Southern Christmas, dark and dank with mist,
And heavy with the scent of steaming leaves,
And rose buds mouldering on the dripping porch;
One twilight, without the rise or set of sun,
Till beetles drone along the hollow lane,
And round the leafless hawthorns, flitting bats
Hawk the pale moths of winter? Welcome then
At best, the flying gleam, the flying shower,
The rain-pools glittering on the long white roads,
And shadows sweeping on from down to down
Before the salt Atlantic gale; yet to come
In whatsoever garb, or gay, or sad,
Come fair or fowl, 'twill still be Christmas Day.[49]

1870s The Kissing Bush in Bideford

In 1928 a resident of Bideford reminisced about the celebrations of Christmas he knew from some fifty years before. He wrote:

The day before Christmas all the gardeners – and there were a good number – were set to work in decorating the entrance and servants' hall with evergreens and holly. In the latter place there used to be hung a huge Christmas Bush. It was the shape of a basin, hanging down from the centre of the ceiling. It would measure, I should think, quite five or six feet in diameter, and would take a good horse load of holly and evergreens to make it complete, and was known as the Christmas or Kissing Bush. The indoor staff used to be kept busy making toast and ale – hot spiced beer – with pieces of dried toasted bread – placed in it. This was free to all-comers during the festive season.

Christmas morning all the farm hands and gardeners used to attend for a hearty attack on the toast and ale. All the men workers on the estate with their wives were invited to dinner, which was served in the servants' hall at mid-day – a meal of roast beef, vegetables, plum-pudding, ale, etc. After tea songs were sung and dancing would take place until 10 o'clock, when hot punch used to be supplied to finish a 'perfect day'.

Another kind of Christmas Bush was one made of two hoops, one placed within the other, which would then be of a globe or orange shape, decorated with holly, mistletoe and evergreens and hung up in a prominent place. The frame of a similar Bush, which is decorated by the inmates, has for 40 years been hung at Christmas time by the Master in the Entrance Lobby of the Bideford Poor-law Institution.[50]

1874 A caution against wishing for a White Christmas

An editorial in *The Devon Weekly Times* cautioned prosperous readers not to wish for snow at Christmas.

Christmas is close upon us. Politically we are at the dead season of the year; but the preparation for celebrating the great festival induces activity among the various industries of the Kingdom. And it is not the decorated shop windows, with their display of 'creature comforts' and beautiful specimens of the manufactures' art, nor the issue of the special literature that alone herald the approach of Christmas. The weather at present is such as to promise a Christmastide of the olden sort. Storm and tempest have been followed by frost and snow, such as we have not witnessed in recent years in December. The weather, in fact, is what is generally described as 'seasonable'. We hope that this seasonableness may ensure extra benevolence on the part of those who can enjoy the keen and frosty air, and on whom the biting north-easter has no effect beyond invigorating the constitution. For it must be remembered that to the ill-fed, the thinly-clad, and badly housed intense cold is the cause of much suffering and distress. There are additional reasons why the purse strings should be generously loosed at this Christmastide, for from all parts, especially from the manufacturing districts, come reports of men out of work, not now through strikes or quarrels between masters and men, but because the work is not to be done. With much wealth we have much poverty. Let it be the province of the wealthy ones at this festive season to seek out and alleviate some of the sufferings of the poor, so that, not only in the homes of the rich, but in the dwellings of the lowly, there may be rejoicing on Christmas Day.

1867
At the Newton Abbot Union House nearly 300 paupers received a Christmas meal of one pound of beef and one pound of pudding as well as vegetables and beer; the men and boys had dinner in one ward and the women and girls in another.

1874 Budleigh Salterton: mummers, 'niggers' and other singers

Some Christmas celebrations have not survived due to changing sensibilities. A newspaper report, entitled 'Christmas Doings', noted that in Budleigh Salterton:

Notwithstanding the dullness of the season and many houses without inhabitants, the people generally have entered into the festivities of Christmas with remarkable ardour. Touched with feelings of tenderest sympathy, the hand of benevolence has

1868
On Christmas Eve two drunken men broke panes of glass in a baker's shop in Teignmouth.

1869
There were a few hitches to the opening on Christmas Eve of 'Number Nip, or Harlequin and the Gnome King of the Giant Mountains', the pantomime at Exeter.

1870
The most popular game at Littlehempston's Christmas Treat was called 'The Postman'.

1871
Primroses were picked in Ipplepen hedgerows.

been stretched forth liberally, and the poor have had reason to rejoice and be glad. Merrily, cheerily rang the bells on Christmas Eve calling upon the parishioners to cast dull care away and enter into joyful spirit into the customary amusements. Bands of juvenile singers, young men and maidens imitating the ancient waits, went from terrace to park carolling their Christmas anthems. Mummer lads in eastern and continental costumes and armed to the teeth with dangerous weapons asserting their right to rule over each other endeavoured to show how battles were fought and won in any house before any assembly who would receive and listen to them, and who would not forget to reward them at its conclusions. Niggers, too, with blackened faces and frizzy polls were singing in Negro patois their war songs, and otherwise imitating them by dancing in the moonlight. Invitations to come and sup had been sent forth to their neighbours and friends by many a well-to-do housekeeper; many a bygone incident was brought up, many an ancient story told of the wonders performed in the 'good old times'. As hour by hour the clock struck, it tolled one more in number, and as the inner man had been replenished again and again, and the cider and malt liquor had given place to something stronger, and as the faces began to heat and a redness over the nose, the singing powers were called into requisition. Song after song with chorus was sung until, as the clock struck again, it struck eleven less than it did the hour before, which was a signal that it would soon be time to depart, with a hearty shake of the hand, therefore, and the wish for a 'Merry Christmas and Happy New Year' friends and neighbours retired to their respective habitations. Names could be mentioned but that may not be. On Christmas Day service was held in the Church and at "The Temple'. In the evening Mr J. Gush entertained 40 boys, members of his Sunday evening class, to tea, after which an address was given them by W. Halstead, Esquire. An interesting evening was spent and the boys went home with merry hearts and laughing faces. Boxing Day, the whole place ran revel, every one did what he considered right in his own eyes, with mummers, niggers, singers, dancers, &c, a repetition of Christmas Eve performances. Thus, without any disorderly cases to report, passed away the Christmas festivities of the present year.[51]

1875 The Christmas Tree

The Victorian Christmas Tree was used as a device to raise funds for good causes. In 1875 a report in *The Devon Weekly Times* noted that:

The 'Christmas Tree' is an institution which rivals the bazaar as a successful means of raising money for charitable and religious purposes; and when the two are combined, the effect is correspondingly greater. The tree and bazaar are therefore very popular just now, especially with those associations – religious and otherwise – which depend on the voluntary principle for their pecuniary support; and so many are got up that one is almost inclined to wonder first where the materials for furnishing trees and stalls come from, and next how it comes that they are all so freely patronised at a time when there is such keen competition going on for loose cash. One explanation may be found in the fact that Christmas trees – rather, the mode of disposing of their burdens, and the ingenious etceteras which generally go along with them – afford some scope for a good deal of fun to those whom the Pantomime and 'such things' are tabooed. They also give the young folk opportunities for flirtation in a mild way; while to 'heads of families' they present an excuse for giving the little ones a treat, with the prospect of something 'nice' to carry home for use or admiration when Christmas-tide, with its delights and cares, its feastings and head-aches, shall once more have become 'a thing of the past'.[52]

1875 A'gooding at Crediton

The practice of a'gooding continued at Crediton at least through the 1870s. It was reported that:

On Christmas Eve B.W. Cleave Esquire, gave 2s 6d to 10s to anyone who went a'gooding to Newcombe House. The entrance gate was thrown open, and as the numerous visitors came up the worthy squire welcomed them with a smiling countenance and his bag of money. People said the Squire could not have given much less than £50 on that blessed Eve. The other members of the Cleave family are of the same generous temperament. There are many other gentlemen and ladies who distribute money &c. according to their means, on this Christmas festival. To add to the pleasures of the time the tradesman's band moved about the parish and played capital selections of music at the gentlemen's residences, as did the Engineer band on Christmas morning. The bells of Holy Cross also rang out merrily. The parish church was tastefully decorated. The choir rendered 'O Zion that bringest good tidings' very creditably.[53]

1875 A gassy Christmas at Newton Abbot

Christmas in Newton Abbot in 1875 does not appear to have been very pleasant judging from a report in the local press.

Keeping Christmas

On Christmas Eve what the *ployès* at the Gas Works were about we don't know, but somehow instead of pumping gas they pumped a mixture into the pipes, so that on Christmas night no gas could be obtained, nothing but a continual fizzing of foul air, and the whole town was in a state of semi-darkness. The annoyance, not only in the streets but also in private dwellings, was considerable, but nothing comparable to that experienced in the churches and chapels where, although a hundred or more jets were burning, or rather fizzing, one another's features could not be distinguished – the singers couldn't see to sing, or the preachers to read or preach, without the aid of candles. The light of an ordinary composite was as a brilliant luminary in the midst of numerous minor satellites. This was the most serious mishap, but not the only one, that has recently occurred at the Gas Works, and a special meeting of the Directors was held on Wednesday to inquire into the matter, and if possible prevent a reoccurrence of it in future.

1875 Moretonhampstead

The following newspaper report by 'T.B.M.E.T' provides an unusually detailed glimpse of Christmas on the edge of Dartmoor.

Moretonhampstead

One could hardly realise that Christmas was come, while feeling slightly oppressed by the sun's rays through the window of the parish church. It seemed so much more like summer than winter that had it not been for the time-honoured customs – the sweet carols of Christmas Eve, the evergreen and holly, the good wishes heard, it might not have been thought that the grand Christian festival was indeed come. Thirteen or fourteen years ago I remember being at Otterton to spend Christmas Day, and in the afternoon I went with some friends for a lovely walk through the meadows to Budleigh Salterton. The weather was charming, the sun shining as though he had forgotten himself and though it was midsummer, instead of mid-winter. I feel I must send you some little description of the festivities we have been having all to ourselves in this moorland town. Christmas Eve was observed as it always is in Moreton. At about eleven o'clock select body of church singers traversed the town, starting at the Rectory. I was informed that the anthem was 'the celestial'; at any rate, a well known young gentleman, who I think occasionally lent his services to the choir during the evening, came to me and somewhat naughtily remarked that his 'celestial' was sure to be in request, after so much dry work at singing. I need scarcely remark what he had in his breast pocket further than to say that when he moved his coat, a large cork came prominently in sight, suggestive of a bottle. The choir acquitted themselves very creditably indeed, the instrumental portion being admirably well rendered by Mr Sanders junior (the harmonium), and Mr F. Trace (the flute). Stopping at the door of the curate (the Rev. W. Francis), the choir at the conclusion of the anthem were greeted with the 'compliments of the season' which were heartily returned. When I say that the Rev. W. Francis is immensely popular with the townspeople, I put the fact in a very mild form. It seems to me that he is the right man in the right place – that he is in fact a man after the parishioners own hearts. He has been mainly instrumental in getting the Church properly warmed, and also getting in the gas. A little stir was made a while since by the publication of an article in the Parish magazine 'Where God has his Church, the Devil will have his –' but the good sense of the parishioners soon told them that the Curate was not answerable for the article, for as he pointed out in the next number, he was only responsible for the local matter. He expressed his regret that it should ever have occurred, and repudiated the tone of the whole article. That, sir, it must be held was manly. Mr Francis is for peace and good will, and the parishioners have show how heartily they appreciate his efforts to secure a good understanding between Church and Chapel. I take this opportunity of saying this, for I saw a complaint from a 'Nonconformist' in your paper, with respect to the article, and have not seen a reply. I must now return to the carols, and in doing so must not forget the beautiful singing of the Wesleyans. 'Rome' got in for it somewhat severely; our Wesleyan friends sang that they were determined that 'Rome' shouldn't delude people – that 'Rome' should fall! 'That's hot', said one friend who was listening; 'No more than they deserve', replied another. Whenever the Wesleyan choir stopped, the leader (Mr Medland) wished the good folks of the house a 'Merry Christmas'. The singing was not over until five o'clock on Christmas morning. I went to church at eleven and was much gratified to observe with how much taste the church had been decorated. Over the altar was the word 'Emmanuel' on a ground of evergreen, holly and moss, and on each side a red cross on a white banner. The pulpit and lectern were tastefully trimmed, and the font reflected very great credit on the ladies who gave so much time to it. Mrs Clack, Mrs Francis, Mr and Mrs Evans, Miss Ribil and others gave their services, and deserve great praise for the success of their efforts. the other places of worship were appropriately decorated, I am told, but I was unable to see for myself. On Monday our band discoursed some good music in the town, and though under some disadvantages, performed their duties highly satisfactorily...

On Tuesday evening we had a grand concert in the Smethurst Schoolroom. The Hall was crowded, and the performances passed off with great satisfaction to all. Several friends from Chagford rendered valuable aid, among them being the Misses Thorn (2), Dr Hunt, Messrs Hurrell and Reed. The Misses Thorn especially came in for a good share of applause – the encores being frequent. Mr Hurrell's services as accompanist were highly successful. The concert was a great success, and must have been very encouraging to its promoters. The Rev. H. Francis, at the close,

1872

On Christmas night a thief stole five rabbits, two cheeses and a bladder of lard from a house in Uplyme.

1873

Sarah Hartnoll of Teignmouth was fined twenty shillings for using obscene language in the streets on Christmas night.

1874

The South Molton fire engines were called out on Christmas Day due to a couple who, while cooking the goose they won in a raffle, had the gravy ignited causing a chimney fire.

1875

Crediton church was decorated with wreaths of variegated holly, ivy, evergreens and flowers.

cordially thanked the Chagford friends who had so kindly lent their services that evening. He hoped at some future time the Moreton friends would be able to return the compliment.

I cannot conclude my letter without a word or two respecting the 'shambles' which for so many years has been a nuisance, if not a disgrace, to the town. The 'shambles' as a sort of butchers' market-house, has, no doubt, been of some sort of service, but the fact cannot be concealed that the building was a positive discomfort to the people living near it. Today (Wednesday) it has been pulled down, and great has been the fall thereof! A friend suggests this as a sort of souvenir of the departed 'shambles' – 'Fell at Moreton on Wednesday, December 29th, 1875, the 'Shambles' after a reign of over half a century. It fell amidst the congratulations of many of the townspeople, and but few lament the loss'. The destruction of the 'shambles is a step in the right direction, and it is evident that Moreton is to see better days.

The schools are in course of erection, and it is expected that they will be opened in the autumn of next year.

We have been afflicted with very bad gas, and are only now recovering. It is far from being free from impurities yet, but it is better than it was; the people say 'It was time to have a change'. Really, the smell was horrible and one hardly knew what poisonous stuff one was inhaling. By New Year's Day we hope to be all well again.

The pathway leading to the station is being completed, and the town wants it badly. It would be a valuable improvement, too, if a little more light could be obtained in the same road for it is by no means a pleasant walk of a dark night, especially in the present condition of the roads.[54]

1876 Christmas carols in Ottery St Mary, Winkleigh, Luppitt, Exmouth and Dartmouth

The singing of Christmas carols was not always well-received as a news report of 1876 shows.

Ottery St Mary

The choir of the Independent Chapel perambulated the town singing Christmas Carols on Christmas Eve and Christmas Night. The church choir did the same.

Winkleigh

The Church and other choirs were about on Christmas Eve, singing carols and anthems in commemoration of the Holy Birth. They were received everywhere in the kindly spirit of the season.

Luppitt

This old and cheerful customs was carried out here on Christmas Eve and Christmas Day by the church choir, and the manner in which they were received everywhere showed that the parishioners were well pleased with the revived custom.

1876

A large whale was seen swimming in Torbay.

Exmouth

Chistmas Eve of this year will be remembered in this town for the number of carols heard in its streets between ten at night and four in the morning, three choirs serenading the inhabitants of the strand, at one time two of them within a dozen yards of each other, in lively competition the discordance being anything but angelic. The Withycombe choir rendered some well-selected anthems with their usual taste and correctness, doing credit to the skilful training under Mr Vinnicombe the organist.

Dartmouth

The time-honoured customs of carol singing was as usual observed in this sacred commemoration. Great disgust and surprise were evinced by the inhabitants at the laxity of the police in permitting such gatherings of rowdiness to annoy the singers and decent people with their coarse language and gross obscenities. A mob of half-drunken sailors and others, wandered through the town and under the pretext of caroling, were singing vulgar songs and passing such ribald jokes as were a disgrace to the place and time.[55]

1876 Old Christmas Day in Torquay

Miss Pinchard, a resident of Tormohun in Torquay, recorded the celebrations on the 6th of January, formerly old Christmas Day, in the nineteenth century. She wrote:

A few years ago, hearing that the ceremony of 'blessing the apple-trees' had been celebrated a night or two before in an orchard close to my house, in the parish of Tormohun, I sent for one of the party who had been officially engaged in the affair to tall me all particulars concerning it.

He told me that, after partaking of a good supper provided by the owner of the orchard, they all, men, women and children, proceeded to the orchard, carrying with them a supply of bread, cheese and cider. They then, all being assembled under one of the best apple-trees, hoisted a little boy up and seated him on a branch. He, it seems, was to represent a tom-tit, and sat there crying out: 'Tit, tit; more to eat'; on which some of the bread and cheese and cider was handed up to

1877
The pantomimes at Exeter were 'Little Red Riding Hood' and 'Little Bo Peep'.

him. He still sitting in the tree, the whole part stood round, each being provided with a little cup, which was forthwith filled with cider, and they then sang the following toast:

> Here's to thee, good apple tree,
> To bear and blow, apples enow,
> This year, next year, and the year after too;
> Hats full, caps full, three-bushel bags full,
> And pay the farmer well.

They then drank all round and fired a salute to the trees, making as much noise as possible with all the pistols, guns or other old firearms they could collect; or, failing such, with explosions of gunpowder placed in holes bored in pieces of wood, accompanying the salute with loud cheering, and then firing into the branches of the trees.

> They then again stood round, and, after another cup of cider, sang:
> To your wassail, and my wassail,
> And joy be to our jolly wassail.

which concluded the ceremony. This was done in dead of winter, and in some cases, buckets of cider with roasted apples floating in them are carried out, and the apple-trees pelted with the apples; but I am not sure whether he said this was done on the occasion of which I write.[56]

1878 Burning the ashen faggot

P.F.S. Amery of Ashburton responded to the reminiscences of William Pengelly by recording his own celebrations.[57] Mr Pengelly had written that the custom of burning ashen faggots had died out in Torquay but in Ashburton the practice continued. Mr Amery acquired his knowledge from an unlikely source: the local rural postmen had noticed while on their rounds that 32 farms and cottages were burning ash faggots on Christmas Eve.

Of the olden customs, so many of which are dying out, that of burning an 'Ashen Faggot' on Christmas-eve still holds it own, and is kept up at many farmhouses.

And well may our Christmas sires of old
Loved when the year its course had rolled,
And brought blithe Christmas back again,
With all its hospitable train,
Domestic and religious rite
Gave honour to the hold night.

Among the various gleanings of the Devon Association Folk-lore Committee is recorded a notice of this custom. We are there informed that on Christmas-eve, 1878, the customary faggot was burned at thirty-two farms and cottages in the Ashburton postal district alone.

The details of the observances vary in different families, but some being common to all, may be considered as held necessary to the due performance of the rite. For example, the faggot must contain as large a log of ash as possible, usually the trunk of a tree, remnants of which are supposed to continue smouldering on the hearth the whole of the twelve days of Christmas. This is the Yule log of our forefathers, from which a fire can be raised by the aid of a pair of bellows, at any moment, day or night, in token of the ancient custom of open hospitality at such a season. Then the faggot must be bound together with as many binders of twisted hazel as possible. Remembering that the ash and hazel were sacred trees with the Scandinavians, their combined presence in forming the faggot may once have contained some mystic signification. Also, as each binder is burned through, a quart of cider is 'craved' by the company. While the fire lasts all sorts of amusements are indulged in, all distinction between master and servant, neighbour and visitor, is for the time set aside.

The heir with roses in his shoes,
That night might village partner choose
The lord, underogating, share
The vulgar game of 'post and pair'
All hailed, with uncontrolled delight,
And general voice, the happy night,
That to the cottage, as the crown,
Brought tidings of salvation down.

In some houses, when the faggot begins to burn up, a young boy is placed on it, and his future pluck foretold by his nerve or timidity. May not this be a remnant of the dedication of children to the deity by passing them through the sacred fire!

Different reasons are given for burning ash. By some it is said that when our Saviour was born, Joseph cut a bundle of ash, which, everyone knows, burns very well when green. With this he lighted a fire, by which the child was first dressed in swaddling clothes.

The gipsies have a legend that our Saviour was born out in the field like themselves, and brought up by an ash fire. The ivy, holly and pine, they say, hid him, and so now are always green, whilst the ash and oak showed where he was hiding, and they remain dead all the winter. Therefore the gipsies burn ash at Christmas.[58]

1878
Choirs from various churches sang carols throughout Winkleigh on Christmas Eve.

1879
On Christmas Night fire destroyed the Ship Inn at Axmouth, caused by the upsetting of a benzoline lamp in the cellar.

1879 Barrack decorations at Devonport

The servicemen at Devonport made special efforts to decorate their barracks for Christmas as a report in the local newspaper noted.

The troops quartered in the town were also enabled thoroughly to enjoy themselves. The men of A Barrery, 1st Brigade, R.A., quartered in Granby Barracks, numbering about 150, were well feasted on roast beef, geese, turkeys and the inevitable plum pudding. The barrack-rooms were neatly decorated by several of the non-commissioned officers, foremost amongst whom were Sergeant Eden and Corporal Little. In the afternoon the barracks were thrown open to the friends of the men, and in the evening there was a dance in the barrack room. The men of the 8th brigade R.A., located at Mount Wise, were similarly treated. The Army Service Corps, stationed in Granby Barracks, dealt with their barrack room in the most elaborate manner. For weeks past several members of the corps, notably Sergeant Major Partridge and Sergeant Howell, assisted by Privates F. Evans, Mills, Ellis and Ware, have been engaged in perfecting a series of decorations and illuminations, made entirely out of coloured paper, and these when lit up in the evening were exceedingly pretty and effective. Some of the illuminations were quite works of art. Upon the windows were comic sketches cut out in tinted paper, and over the main entrance was an illuminated clock, the handiwork of the sergeant-major. Military mottoes and devices were very plentiful upon the walls, whilst each corner of the room was lit up with a transparency. Sergeant Howell executed these, and also a water-colour sketch of a team and wagon in the marching order of the Army Services Corps. The finest piece of work occupied the centre of the ceiling. It was a representation of the wheel of life, and was composed of just 2,000 pieces of coloured paper. This, also, was the work of the sergeant-major. A paper model of the Eddystone, with a passing vessel in full sail, executed by Privates Mills and Ellis; and a transparent model of the block of buildings occupied by the corps, the design of Sergeant Howell, were among the other ornamentations of the room. In this apartment the men were feasted.[59]

1879 Christmas in Plymouth's shops

The goods on sale in shops were a seasonal Victorian attraction as this report in *The Western Morning News* shows:

The requisite fur, the seasonable 'beaver' and maybe the indispensable umbrella, for a continuance of the Christmas ramble, may be chosen at Mr T.W. Lansdown's Bedford House, where, too, shopping *ab. lib.* in seasonable gifts is invited. An addition of some movement to the ladies during the muddy season will be one of Allen's overlasting dress protectors, which forms a waterproof and dirtproof lining for the exposed edge of the dress. It is a Plymouth designed article, and is becoming as popular as it is useful. In Old Town Street, passing on from the *habitat* of the 'Victoria' jersey, at Lancaster and Co.'s, the first important display is that of Messrs. Stidston, Moulder and Stidston, an establishment where a complete outfit for either sex may be had, while fancy goods of Japanese, German, French and English invention are offered. The show of *immortelles* and grasses at Mr Steward's is unique and in brightness and variety quite merits inspection. For all the prettiest ribbons of the season step across to Mr E. Keen's. Mr Ellis's large stock of gold and silver wares is sterling in quality and tastefully arranged. With now confectionary and bon-bons, anon Christmas cards and next year's calendars, past Messrs Yabsley's and Messrs. Rendle and Co.'s luxurious house furniture, and, with a glance at Mr Chamber's fanciful confectionary, Christmas fruit is seen to advantage at Lloyd's and Waring's. Thousands of pounds of grapes tempt paterfamilias, as well as countless golden-orbed oranges, but English boys and girls will be sorry to hear that with all the wealth of superior foreign fruit there are no homemade productions to be had. The English apple, like the English summer, is *non est inventus* this year. Treville Street will no doubt, repay a ramble by-and-bye as far as Mill's bazaar of varieties. In Whimple Street, again Mr Cox's wonder-working electro processes fill two brilliantly lit windows with modern gold and silver. Nor should a visit to Mr Trythall's stationery depot in Old Town Street be omitted. Besides the productions of the English makers of cards, the Continental artists, whose work on satin makes this year's Christmas tokens so durable, furnish new designs adapted to mythical as well as sculptural mottoes. Perry's revolving album, a glass case swung upon ornamental uprights, which, by a very simple arrangement, brings fifty-two portraits successively to view, is the newest thing in stationery. Mr J. Smith, Old Town Street, also shows Christmas stationery.

Bedford Street brings us by interesting stages to Mr H. Matthews', where confectionary of all kinds, from the plum cakes of the story books to deftly-fashioned Twelfth Cakes, which are real works of art, is shown here in the greatest variety. The corner below, ablaze as it is with light, brings the almost-deserted 'island' into by no means festive relief. The tenants have begun to move into these new premises. Plate and jewellery, in designs adapted to Christmas gifts, are seen at Mr Boney's; and Messrs. Searle call attention not only to their superior assortment of this class of work, but to a large army of clocks – no doubt including that popular, but antiquated specimen, 'Grandfather's Clock', which, with the music of the song engraved on it, furnishes several designs in fancy goods elsewhere. McBryde Brothers, as a new firm, are able to set off their window with the latest fashions in haberdashery.

At the head of George Street is the establishment of the local Worth – Mr H. Barons – where, as always, rich taste in costumery is evidenced by a few well-selected costumes. Messrs. Moon will fascinate many of the passers-by with a novelty in musical-boxes – a Swiss production, the mechanism of which sets a curiously combined landscape in motion. 'Birdies Roll-Call' and the rest of the new Christmas music, with the most cheerful of frontispieces, with music in classic bindings, specially prepared for Christmas presents, are what Messrs. Moon really desire

1880

The Mayor of Biddeford revived an ancient custom by attending church service with the Town Clerk and Council on Christmas Day.

1881
There was dense fog in Newton Abbot on Christmas Day.

attention for however. One excellent idea is a musical Christmas card. At Mr Hawke's studio unrivalled *cartes de viste* have for the time [being] given place to excellent Christmas cards, with which, inside a long gallery is completely garnished. The value of the stock is upwards of £500. Mr Burnard's old-established fancy depot is making its last Christmas season. Across the way some choice productions in the fashionable styles of millinery occupy Mrs Prattent's window space. A new and convenient showroom at the rear, which has been judiciously exchanged for unnecessary breadth of frontage, contains the novelties of the season, of which the chief are the Grecian wealth, an effective headdress in coral tints, and novel pink and scarlet garnitures in very natural geraniums. Mr Walkey carries out a good idea in the way of Christmas boxes, boxes for which he makes ample provision in ornamental as well as pretty 'sets' to fill them. Artificial flowers, particularly holly and mistletoe, also invite the judgment of the ladies. Messrs Sawday and Co. yield to no one in variety or seasonableness of their Christmas presents in a musical way. Messrs. Spearman and Spearman maintain their recognised high position as mercers by an extensive stock in which the season's novelties hold the prominent places. Fur-lined cloaks, in what may be called the *edition de luxe* of that class of goods, and among innumerable other products of the loom, the Scotch 'maude' of which we recently heard so much, are the distinctive line of business. Messrs. Bowering and Co. supplement their ordinarily large stock of books and stationery, with Christmas and New Year cards, of which they make up convenient assortments at suitable prices. While it would be unkind to suggest 'glasses', Messrs. Heath and Bullingham fairly claim attention for their photographic trophies, which are as suitable mementoes as pictorial cards.

Going by way of Bank of England Place to Union Street, Mr G.R. Baratt's India-rubber dolls and other indestructible toys lure the unwary to the examination, not only of the toys, but of winter waterproofs and other indispensables. Mr H.M. Harris puts his customers in the way of providing handsome Christmas gifts for themselves, not only emblematic cards suited to their own particular circumstances, but painted china even, a branch of art work which has become so popular that presents of the 'tools' may well be made. The remarkable pair of pictures, 'The First Easter Dawn' and 'The First Christmas Morning' by Mr J.K. Thompson, which Mr Harris is showing in reduced sizes, also form a very suitable gift. Mr Gaylard, the proprietor of one of the largest stocks of toys in the Western Counties, lays himself out to suit every imaginable taste in the way of toys, curiosities, keepsakes, and miscellaneous useful goods. 'The Dirty Boy' and the soap he was washed with are among the specialties. The 'Emporium' justifies its name with a collection of gifts, mementoes, and toys in all possible materials. A good collection of terra-cotta is included here. Traversing Union Street several good things are seen, but one of the most striking is the improvement effected by Mr Seymour, at No. 1 and the adjoining premises. The large structural improvement is fully utilised by the attractive show of drapery it facilitates. The adjoining premises, occupied by Mr R.G. Lake, outfitter, and Mr A. Kent, toy dealer, also improve upon the improvement. On the way back Messrs. E.A. Lake and Co.'s outfitting establishment deserves a visit. Not only immense stores of ready-made clothing, but valuable Christmas presents, including works of art and literature, personal ornaments and pictures, toys and tea.

These notes must not be understood to exhaust the round of Christmas sensations. In Mount Pleasant Terrace, for example, at the agency of the Torquay Terra Cotta Company, Eddystone plaques and other local ideas suggest themselves as presents. In Cornwall Street our Cornish cousins are suitably enough invited by Mr Southcombe to select their Christmassing' from a large stock of drapery. At Mr J. Burt's ladies caps and fancy goods are a specialty. For old-fashioned shows of Christmas goods some of the bye streets also compete to advantage.[60]

1882
'Robinson Crusoe' was Exeter's pantomime.

1881 Devonshire Christmas-tide customs

In 1881 William Crossing, the writer on Dartmoor, reminisced about Christmas in Devon. He wrote:

Many of the old customs connected with Christmas have now almost, if not entirely, disappeared.

The ceremony of wassailing the apple trees' in former days, was often observed in the cider districts of Devonshire, and was kept sometimes on Christmas Eve and sometimes on Twelfth Day-eve. The best bearing tree in the orchard was generally selected as the one round which the ceremony was performed, and after its health was duly drank in cider, and some of the same beverage sprinkled over its roots, a song, commencing 'Here's to thee, old Apple-tree' was sung and cheers given by the farmer and his men, who left the orchard with a firm conviction that there would be a plentiful bearing of apples in the coming year. A full account of this interesting observance may be found in Mrs Whitcombe's *Bygone Days in Devonshire and Cornwall*.

Burning the Yule log and the faggot of ash are customs now more honoured in the breach than in the observance, and the old Devonshire 'Christmas Play' is entirely a thing of the past. The ancient custom of 'Watching the Pie' was doubtless observed in former times in the southern part of our county, as Herrick, who was vicar of Dean Prior towards the middle of the seventeenth century, mentions it. The pie was supposed to represent the manger in which our Lord was laid, and the contents of it the offerings of the Wise Men. The ceremony consisted of its being watched and guarded by the person all through the night before Christmas. The custom of the old women of the parish 'going a-gooding', as it is termed, we still find kept up. This consists of their going round to the houses of their more wealthy neighbours for small donations of money, or other gifts; and the carol singers still

1883
Fire broke out in the Exeter Inn at Honiton.

pay us their visits, this early custom flourishing as in the days of yore, when the minstrels sought the holly-decked hall of the feudal baron, and with pipe and tabor made 'sweet music' gladdening the hearts of young and old, and ushering in the festive season of Merry Christmas.[61]

1883 Christmas in Ilfracombe, Exmouth, Okehampton, Bradninch, Exeter and Plymouth

The Western Times reported very different experiences of Christmas for six places in Devon with two reports of a clash at Exeter between opposing cultures.

Ilfracombe

On Friday evening [27 December] a procession was formed in Broad Street, and an effigy was hoisted on the shoulders of a youth. It started in the direction of Fore Street and High Street accompanied by a mob of several hundred persons singing songs and ringing hand bells. After traversing the higher parts of the town the procession returned to the Strand where the effigy was burnt in the presence of a large concourse of people.

Exmouth

Christmas on the outside has been dull in the extreme in this town, as well as in all other parts of our Island Home, but barring the weather, the season and the opportunity for family gatherings have been enjoyed with as much relish as ever. Fishermen have had a quiet time of it during the last few nights on account of the dense fogs prevailing. On Christmas Eve a few venturesome boats went out and got some fish but the coming in was quite another matter. One of them, belonging to Mr Hooper, got on the Maer Rocks, and although she did not receive much damage, she had to remain until she got more water and more light. An Exmouth boat bringing home a passenger from Starcross got so befogged that the Christmas Eve was spent somewhere between Bulhill and the Bight. After some hours of speculative pulling, father and son got hold of a buoy, and by dint of an illumination, got up between them, managed to make out the number of the 'Bight's Buoy' and by careful steering got home about midnight. Christmas Eve of 83 will be remembered by that passenger to the end of his life. Carollers were not as numerous as on former occasions – whether they also got lost in the fog is unknown.

1884

The talk in Crediton was of a pig found down a baker's well.

Okehampton

On Christmas Day evening service was held in the parish church on the occasion of its being lit with gas for the first time.

Bradninch

On Friday last Mrs John Sharland, a lady alike noted for her age (being a lady of 96 summers and the oldest inhabitant of Bradninch) and her liberality observed the customs, which she has practised for a great number of years, of giving three-penny pieces on St Thomas's Day to all the deserving poor who call at her door and ask for it. The benevolent old lady might be seen throughout the day answering the door herself, with a cheery smile for each applicant and her activity and vigour at her advanced age sets a good example to many much younger than herself.

Exeter

The Salvation Army observed the Christmas with services described in their usual emphatic language. There was 'breakfast with the Lord' at the hall on the Friars, after which the band marched through the streets, and there was a holiness meeting. In the afternoon the 'troops' met 'on the old battlefield, at the bottom of Paris Street, and after a skirmish with the enemy, the Devonshire regiment marched to the Temple, where volunteers took part in a 'free-and-easy.' There was subsequently a tea, followed by a march round the City, and then a meeting at the hall. The services were led by Captain Taylor, assisted by two Lieutenants, and there were large attendances.

James Paul, labourer, was charged with being in a company of roughs in High Street, fighting with another young man in front of the Salvation Army near the South Street Crossing, when PC Dymond took him in custody and brought him to the Station. PC Wheeler also gave evidence of the fight, the disorderly crowd, and the dispersion of the Salvation Army. It was shown that he had been before the court more than 15 times. Fined 5s and costs, or seven days in prison.[62]

Plymouth

Christmas morning at the Devon and Cornwall Female Orphan Asylum was observed with the usual discipline yesterday. The inmates went to church before dinner, and again in the afternoon. During the day Miss Cooke presented each girl with a Christmas card; a supply of wool mittens was sent anonymously from London and the Treasurer, Mr F.H. Goulding, gave each child a new shilling. After tea every restriction was withdrawn and the inmates indulged in innocent amusement. The Christmas tree and entertainment will take place during next week.[63]

1885
A few days after Christmas the Bishop of Exeter preached a sermon to two thousand children in the Cathedral.

1883 People who don't keep Christmas

On Boxing Day the *Western Morning News* reminded its readers of the labour cost of Christmas.

Some people don't keep Christmas because they won't and others because they can't. Among the former must, we suppose, be reckoned 'Jews, Turks and infidels' and – we hope the association will not be thought disrespectful – the Society of Friends. Those who would keep Christmas if they could but are unable are for the most part servants of that inexorable taskmaster, the Public. Of course all who work with hand or head for a livelihood, from the mason's labourer, whose remuneration is at the rate of 4d an hour, to the bank manager who draws a handsome stipend, are performing, in their several spheres, a duty to society; and in that indirect means are public servants. But it is not of these we speak. It is of persons – and they are far more numerous than the unobservant might suppose – who minister directly to the wants of the public or are responsible for its safety. The vast majority of this class, far from being able to participate in the pleasures of the multitude are compelled by reason of that very devotion to enjoyment on the part of their more fortunate fellows to work harder than they would be otherwise entitled. And while hundreds of persons are ready to flood the daily journals with appeals for an additional twenty-four hours relaxation from business to enable shop assistants to keep an extended holiday, few, indeed, are the words of sympathy heard from those who from force of circumstances are unable to observe even Christmas Day as a holiday; or, what is perhaps worse, have to forego the pittance upon which the daily fare of their family depends in order to 'enjoy' a compulsory and unwelcome respite from work.

The Plymouth police force, for instance, is a good example of a body of men whose duty, collectively, never ends. From week to week, month to month, year to year, decade to decade, the Plymouth streets are patrolled without intermission by the guardians of peace and order, and it follows, no matter now judicious the division of labour, the policeman's enjoyment of Christmas can be but very partial and unsatisfactory. The officers employed in watching the borough number in all 91. At nine o'clock on Christmas Eve 39 of these men were placed upon their respective beats where they stayed through 'the middle watches of the night' until six o'clock on Christmas morning, when they were relieved by twelve constables, who remained on duty for three hours. These, in their turn, were relieved at 9 am by fifteen constables, and at 1 pm another interchange between the two sets took place. At 4 o'clock the afternoon detachment went home for tea for one hour, and from 5 until 9 pm the two day staffs perambulated the town conjointly, when the night policemen were again posted for another nine hours melancholy ramble. In addition to these forces there are a certain few reserve men, always ready to supply any deficiency in the ranks or undertake any special work, with of course a proportionate number of inspectors and sergeants. This is the ordinary routine of a policeman's duty, and a somewhat similar arrangement exists at Devonport, and of course in all other towns of considerable size. Can it be said that any of the ninety-one men thus employed by the town are able to enjoy Christmas? Certainly not those who remain the whole night in the streets, because for at least six or seven hours on Christmas Day they must be sleeping in order to fit themselves to return to their respective beats at nine o'clock; and certainly not those who are unable to spend more than four consecutive hours at home on the great feast day.

But while a policeman's lot is not a more happy one at Christmas than at other periods of the year, there are classes upon whom the additional labour involved is very considerable. Think of the Post Office *employés*. How many people in Plymouth to whom the receipt of Christmas cards yesterday brought so much additional pleasure as indications that they were not forgotten by distant friends, or how many of those who heedlessly dropped into the post office similar missives of goodwill and good fellowship, were aware that the pressure entailed upon the postal department by this pleasant custom rendered it necessary that eight clerks and sorters should spend the whole of Christmas Eve and Christmas Day travelling backwards and forwards between Falmouth and Exeter in order to arrange for the delivery at the various towns on the route. Such, however, was the case. Then, again, between 50 and 60 clerks were occupied in similar duties at the General Post Office, Plymouth, from Tuesday morning, on through the night, and only left work yesterday at noon in order to go home and spend the rest of the day in bed. Sixty postmen were in attendance at the central office before six o'clock yesterday morning, and the majority of them were engaged in the pleasing and invigorating exercise of knocking their way through the streets of Plymouth at the rate of a penny a knock from that hour until midday.

The cabmen are another unfortunate class to whom Christmas never comes as a season of enjoyment and relaxation from a round of monotonous labours. There are about 200 public vehicles in the Three Towns, and 200 drivers were more or less occupied from 6.30 yesterday morning until the early hours of this morning ministering with their carriages to the comfort of the opulent. How many of those who rolled home in ease from the family party, from the well-furnished drawing-room, from the feast, from the dance, or it might be from the church, gave a passing thought as to how the man on the box spent his Christmas? How many of those who complacently stirred the milk into their chocolate or coffee at the late breakfast, congratulating themselves on a temporary cessation from labour, and lingering over half a dozen schemes for spending the day, remembered that someone must have been out of bed hours before daylight tending his cattle and delivering the milk, and would have to repeat the same round of duties in the afternoon? Very few, we trow.

Did anyone of the thousands who made merry in their brilliantly-lighted homes last night think once of those forty men, half-stripped and with the perspiration rolling down over their begrimed bodies, who were labouring like so many Vulcans in the lurid glare of the retort-house at Coxside? True, the Gas Company give the men who thus spend their Christmas in the public service additional pay and in this matter set a praiseworthy example. But the men lose their holiday. They must lose it. The exigencies of their position demand that they shall do so. Theirs is a labour which, like the policeman's, never ceases, and one gang only goes on duty to relieve another. A very large class to whom Christmas only comes as a season of

1886

A mild Christmas Day was followed on Boxing Day by several days of extreme rain and snow.

1887
On Boxing Day a cedar, two yews and an evergreen oak were planted in Uffculme to mark Queen Victorian's Jubilee.

harder toil are the railway *employés*. There are signalmen living in Plymouth who spend twelve hours out of every twenty-four hauling at the levers and attending to the telegraph instruments in a signal box, and this species of imprisonment goes on all the year round, with, perhaps, a day's holiday every few weeks to vary the monotony. Do these men every compose odes to 'solitude!' or teach spiders and mice acrobatic feats? There are upwards of 100 porters and officials employed at the Great Western Railway Station, Millbay, and the man among them who gets more than six consecutive hours for sleep at Christmas time is regarded among his fellows as one of Fortune's favourites. Roughly speaking, the staff is divided into two gangs – one being on duty from 6 yesterday morning until 2 pm, and the other gang from 2 pm until late at night; but there is no certainty about this rule, and the exceptions are numerous. It is by no means an infrequent occurrence – and there are instance within our knowledge – for men who had, as they fondly hoped, completed a long and laborious day's work, to be sent away in charge of a train or to carry out some duty on another section of the line. To the tramway staff of the Three Towns, also, Christmas is an excessively busy time. The manager of the company (Mr Moreton) has about forty men under his direction, including drivers, conductors, stablemen, and roadmen, and the whole of these were employed in their several capacities from about ten o'clock yesterday morning until ten at night, with two very brief intervals for meals.

But there is yet a class of men to whom Christmas comes as a heavier burden than to any of those previously spoken of. It is the men who, earning the barest possible pittance, are compelled to abstain from work, and to keep a holiday at the cost of a day's pay. Take a pick and shovel labourer, for instance, who has to maintain himself and a wife and half a dozen children upon a princely allowance of 4½d an hour, and who was mulct yesterday to the tune of about 3s 4d because humanity in general was taking a holiday and feasting itself. Does anyone suppose that a man under those circumstances 'keeps' Christmas? One might as well expect him to bring up his family on nectar and ambrosia. We asked a labourer who is employed for nine and a half hours daily in hauling stones to the top of a new public building in Plymouth, and whose remuneration is at the rate named, whether he did not rejoice at the prospect of a holiday. The holiday was well enough, sure, was the reply, but the loss of wages meant that the family would have to go short of victuals at some time or another to make up the deficiency. In fact the man hinted a wish that he could work on Sunday. Shocking, some people who sat down to their turkey with a sherry yesterday would exclaim, but the man was right in one respect. Christmas was no boon to him, rather did it rob his family of bread, and make one day the less on which he could earn his 3s 4d during the hard winter months. We are not moralising; these are the facts, and the same argument applies in a greater or less degree to masons, carpenters, plumbers, and all of those to whom a cessation of work means an ill-afforded stoppage of pay.

It may be thought 'bad form' for a journalist to allude to himself or his class. But journalists are, after all, only human beings, and like holidays quite as much as other people. A newspaper staff has – to speak in nautical phraseology – no 'watch below'. Telegrams and manuscripts have on Christmas evening to be edited and revised, articles have to be written, reporting has to be done, type has to be set, and all the machinery of the newspaper office has to be in full working order on Christmas night in order that the literary meal may be duly served up on the morning of Boxing Day. True, the printer may spend Christmas Eve in bed, if he desires an unwonted luxury, but that is not the evening of Christmas Day, when few can be spared in any department from the nightly round of duties. Clergymen and organists, we suppose, would repudiate the idea that they don't 'Keep Christmas' yet there is a sense in which they must look on the duties of the day as somewhat irksome. There are many others who don't keep Christmas. There are watermen, ferrymen, toll collectors, lighthouse keepers, sentries, sailors, dock keepers, signalmen, barmaids, domestic servants, ostlers, and many others. Our desire has been to say a few words to evoke the sympathy of our readers for these victims of circumstances to whom Christmas only brings its special toils and deprivations. To some of these consolation comes only in the form of a consciousness of having fulfilled the expectation expressed in Lord Nelson's famous Trafalgar signal.[64]

1888
Early on Christmas morning a burglar attempted to rob the Bristol and West of England Bank in Torquay.

1887 Christmas in East Budleigh, Mortehoe, Great Torrington and Upottery

Newspaper reports show the variety of Christmas experiences in 1887.

East Budleigh

A special Christmas entertainment was given in the schoolroom by the 'Wizard of East Devon' (Dr Brushfield) under the name of Magacabalistihankipankiton. The room was filled to overflowing... the audience were delighted with the capital conjuring tricks, and testified their admiration by loud applause. Where all is good it is difficult to single out any trick, but possible the favourite one was 'The marvellous flowers' (Bautier de Kolta's new illusision).

Mortehoe

The interesting old church at Mortehoe, North Devon, has had for centuries a ring of three pre-Reformation bells, one being an *Ave Maria*. Through the liberality of G.B. Longstaff, Esquire, they have been augmented to a peal of six by additional trebles, which bear the crest of the donor and inscriptions *Te Deum Laudamus* and *Venite Audite*. The new ones beautifully harmonise with the old ones. The contract has been carried out by Mr Aggett of Chagford, who has completed the work in a most satisfactory manner.

Great Torrington

A free breakfast was given to about 200 poor children on Monday morning. The breakfast consisted of cake, bread and butter, coffee, &c. The Reverend J. Morrell

1889
On Christmas Eve a window display of a snowstorm in an Exmouth shop caught fire.

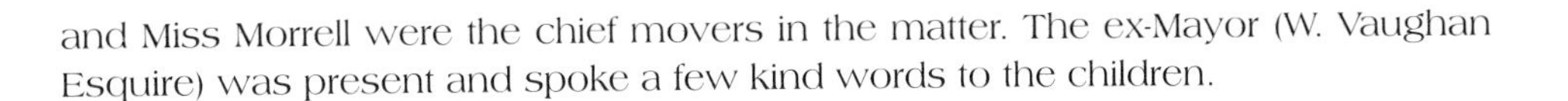

and Miss Morrell were the chief movers in the matter. The ex-Mayor (W. Vaughan Esquire) was present and spoke a few kind words to the children.

Upottery

While the bells were being rung on Christmas Day, a collie dog belonging to Mr Clarke made its way up the staircase and got among the bells, getting its head entangled in the wheel of the tenor, nearly bringing the bell down. The dog is little hurt.[65]

1888 The locals and the navvies at Tavistock

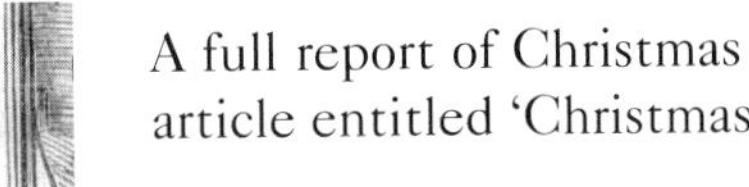

A full report of Christmas in 1888 was printed in Tavistock's local newspaper in an article entitled 'Christmas Tide'.

The Committee of the Cottage Hospital beg to return thanks for the following Christmas presents – a turkey from Mr Radford, dessert from Mr Brodrick, and a cake from Mrs Joseph Browne.

On Christmas Eve the bells rang out merrily, the fife and drum band paraded the streets, and although winter was disagreeably wet, but mild, there were a great number of holiday folk about, and the shopkeepers seemed to be unusually busy. Between four and five on Christmas morning the waits were astir, and later the bells again rang out, and during the day the handbell ringers visited various parts of the town. Wednesday was kept strictly as a bank-holiday. The jewellers announced that they would close from Saturday night until Thursday morning, but for some occult reason the arrangement fell through, and they opened as usual on Monday.

On the morning of Christmas Day service was held in the parish church and in most of the other places of worship in the town excepting the New Church, where service was held the previous evening. Both churches were decorated very ornately, and after service in the parish church, a collection was made in behalf of the fund for the relief of the poor at Christmas, amounting to nearly £8. In the afternoon there was good attendance in the Parish Church, when the first 12 numbers of the Messiah were given, concluding with the Hallelujah Chorus. The musical portion of the service was under the direction of the organist, Mr John Tomlinson.

Through the kindness of many friends the poor of this town have not been forgotten, nor their wants unsupplied during the Christmas. All those receiving outdoor relief and those but a little better off, have received an order for coals, meat and groceries. Those with families have received larger orders. By these means, none of the deserving poor have been overlooked.

Mrs Harry Weight's Theatre is now open at West Bridge. Since Mr Harry Weight's death, Mrs Weight has carried on the theatre, and as the company are old favourites in this town, we are glad to welcome them for the holidays. A pantomime has been produced abounding with fun and frolic, which would be credit to a much larger stage. Clown, Pantaloon, Harlequin and Columbine are well up to their work. The pantomime is preceded each evening by a comic performance.

On Wednesday afternoon an entertainment was given to the Navvies' wives and children, in the Mission Room, which was prettily decorated. About 80 women and 140 children were present. The tea was free, and the people came from Broadwell on one side and Marytavy on the other. There was also a Christmas tree heavily laden with toys and other presents for the children, all of which were given. The evening, which was most pleasantly spent, finished up with singing and some laughable sketches. A good many of the public were present between 3 and 4 o'clock to look at the Christmas Tree. Mr Massey, the Navvy Missioner, desires to return thanks for the many acts of kindness which have been shown towards the Mission during Christmas.[66]

1890
Beef, bacon and cake were taken from the Newfoundland Inn in Newton Abbot.

1889 An Ebeneezer Christmas

In 1889 *The Western Daily Mercury* advertised Boxing Day at the Ebeneezer Schools in Plymouth.

This afternoon and evening the annual Christmas festival will be held. It comprises a 'Christmas Tree' with a long and varied programme of interesting and amusing entertainments. There will be the 'Chanty' fishermen from the Bethel, Mr Rickard, with his ventriloquial entertainment, concerts, magic lantern, &c; also a really good exhibition of rare and valuable curiousities. The room and corridors will be transformed into a veritable fairy land, the effect of an artistic blending of flags, evergreens, pictures, and mirrors being pleasing in the extreme. Refreshments will be provided during the evening at moderate prices, and persons desirous of spending a pleasant evening at a small cost may do so at the Ebeneezer.[67]

1889 Christmas at the Lucky Horseshoe Studio

Harry Hems, the illustrious wood-carver of Exeter, annually entertained a considerable number of poor elderly citizens at Christmas. In 1889 it was reported that it was his 21st year of such hospitality.

The usual festival took place at Mr Harry Hems's Lucky Horseshoe Studios at Longbrook Street, Exeter, when about three score broken-down citizens and their

1891
Heavy rain and fog made Christmas Day gloomy in Plymouth.

wives feasted right royally and literally to their hearts' and stomachs' contents. The gathering took place in one of the large wood-carving workshops, which had been transformed for the nonce from a busy hive of industry into a fine banqueting hall, and was fine decorated. At the higher end of the room was a famous Christmas tree, laden with a crop of more than a hundred gifts, all calculated to make the hearts of children glad. This tree, however, did not come to the old people's share, but is to form one of the main attractions today (Boxing Day), when the children of St Martha's Orphanage and other little ones are to be entertained by the host and his family to a tea and magic lantern. The old people began to assemble soon after one o'clock. The sexes were apparently about equally divided, and some fine old heads and venerable forms graced the tables. Dinner was served at half-past one, and consisted of a prime sirloin of the roast beef of Old England, joints of mutton and pork, and half-a-dozen geese. These were served piping hot with plenty of vegetables and tankards of foaming ale, amongst those who waited upon the venerable guests being the Rev. S.W.E. Bird, rector of the parish, Messrs. Greville, C. and Harry T. Hems, junior, and G.F. Passmore. All the time the three Misses Hems and Miss Florence Jennings rattled away at the piano, and after the more substantial part of the dinner had been done justice to the plum pudding, flanked by light infantry in the shape of a small army of mince pies, appeared upon the scene.

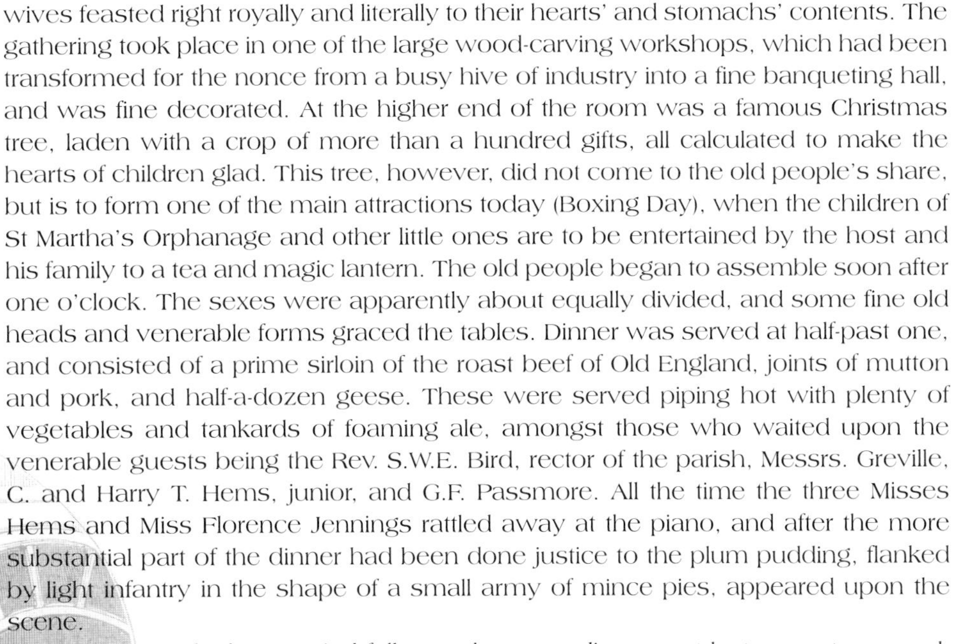

The dinner, which occupied fully two hours to discuss, at last came to an end, when smoking, etc. were the order of the day. Then the Lord Bishop of Exeter entered the room, and was greeted by all present as an old friend. The usual toasts followed, and the health of Mr and Mrs Harry Hems and their large family was proposed and drunk with enthusiasm. Mr Hems, in responding, said this was the twenty-first successive Christmas Day that he had found himself in precisely the same position he now occupied. He had looked back over his old papers and he found that during the period of twenty years he had, by the blessing of God, been enabled to entertain upwards of 1,700 good folks such as themselves. He wished all present a very bright new year.[68]

1889 A Christmas pantomime

In 1889 'Cinderella' played at the Thespian Temple in Plymouth's Union Street. It featured a struggle between Cupid and the Demon King and like all pantomimes of the time it had topical references such as the introduction of electric light and striking workers as well as numerous local ones:

The Pantomime opens with a view of the Demon Forge where the Demon King's minions are discovered at work and the following dialogue takes place between Brimstonio and his imps –

You little imps, what's all this row and riot?
I'll knock your heads off if you don't keep quiet.
Of work today you haven't done a stroke.
And poor Brimstonio is near Brim'stony-broke'.
You haven't made those Sixpenny Sulphur Shockers.

Vesta: No, we're on strike, boss, like the London Dockers.

Vesuvius: We want a penny an hour more.

Brim: Well, I'm sure,
If wages here go up a penny more,
This firm will bust. Your wages no one earns.

Vesta: All right then, come on, mates: let's give him *Burnt*.

Brim: Drop that, you little Demons! I'll soon see,
You imps, you give your imp-udence to me!
Take that, and that. I'll give it to you hot.
Your strike must be, 'Strike while the iron's hot.'
So get to work at once, or quickly this'll –

Imps (subdued) We will obey. (steam horn heard)

Brim: Ah, there goes *Will-obey's* whistle.
'Tis five o'clock – you needn't work any later.
Hi! You Vesuvius, get me a drop of *cratur*.

Brimstonio and dynamite, finding nothing for evil hands to do are about to go in the Stonehouse Workhouse, when they remember that being Christmas time it is their duty to dish the Fairy Queen. Electra, the Fairy Queen, on entering soliloquises thus:

And you will find Electra's radiant rays
Will supercede the light of other days.

(Brim: No more oil lamps.)

Yes, that will come to pass.
No more complaints about the Plymouth gas.
And when you once inaugurate my reign,
The South London gas strikers won't strike again.[69]

1890 The Starcross Asylum children's party

In 1890 the terminology was different but the expression of good will was similar.

Starcross, 1890

The children of the Idiot Asylum, Starcross, had their annual treat and Christmas tree on Tuesday evening in the large hall of the Institution. The hall presented a very attractive appearance with its festoons of evergreens and groups of banners, and lighted by hundreds of fairy and Japanese lamps. Here the guests assembled at 4 o'clock, and after a short address from the Superintendent, Mr W. Locke, the children sang some carols in capital time and tune. Each of the inmates (numbering 190) then received a suitable gift from the tree (a very fine one presented by Mr John Drewe), the ladies [who were] present kindly assisted by dispensing them to the recipients. This was followed by plum cakes and oranges, and much merriment was caused at the explosion of the crackers and the wearing of the fantastic articles found in the bon-bons liberally distributed to the youngsters. After some more carols had been sung, the Superintendent thanked the visitors for their attendance and assistance, and also the donors for their contributions, and stated that he had that morning received a letter from the Honorable Secretary of the Devonshire Doll Show, informing him that the Committee had decided to expend from the surplus funds in hand the sum of £3 for the purchase of toys for the children of Starcross Asylum.[70]

1891 The Robins' treat

During the 1890s Exeter provided an annual treat to some of the city's poorest children who were referred to as 'Robins'.

The Robins' Treat

Exeter fortunately, unlike the larger towns of the Kingdom, has not many children who may properly be described as waifs and strays, but there is a large number, probably not fewer than three thousand, who at this festive season are denied even the sight of the luxuries with which tables in the houses of the well-to-do classes are laden. For these poor children Christmas would have no pleasures were it not for the philanthropic citizens who every year give them treats in various parts of the city. The annual treat to the Robins, as the poor children are termed, took place in the Barnfield Hall last evening. The first of these gatherings was held four years ago in the Lower Market, when about seven hundred children assembled, but the Committee found, as was to be expected, that a more careful plan of selection was necessary if the treat was to be given to those only who were really in need. This year the cases have been closely inquired into, and the result was that the number of children in the hall last evening did not exceed four hundred. It was not necessary to look at the majority of them more than once to see that they had been strangers to the good things of the season. It was, indeed, a motley gathering. They were generally ill-clad, and the cages of many of them seemed to indicate that the application of soap and water would make them more comfortable. But despite these circumstances they were apparently cheerful and happy, their keen eyes watching the boxes of food which were presently opened, and the contents distributed among them. It was evidently one of the happiest moments in their lives. By means of a magic lantern in the gallery the words of that beautiful hymn 'Hark! the herald angels sing' were thrown on a large screen in front of the children, who joined in singing it heartily, after which Mr H. Gadd, JP, ascended the platform and delivered an appropriate address explaining the meaning of the great Christian festival, and giving them much excellent advice. Then the feast commenced. The food did not consist of meat, which, the Committee have found by experience, does the children harm owing to the fact that they take a surfeit; but of buns and hot milk. After having their hunger appeased they were treated to a magic lantern entertainment by Mr Louis Honey. Each child before leaving was given a packet of food and garments. Included in each parcel was a packet of tea to be taken home as a present for the mother. Before separating the National Anthem was sung.[71]

1892
The newly-formed troupe of 'Amateur Darkies' played on Boxing Day in Topsham.

1892 A Plymouth turkey

The *Western Daily Mercury* noted an unusually heavy turkey in 1892.

A Plymouth householder's Christmas experience prompts him to ask whether the farmers of Devon and Cornwall have heard of the latest remedy for agricultural depression. We are told, he says, that corn can no longer be grown at a profit, that beef and mutton are poor reeds to lean upon, and that the British farmer must look

1893
Seven members of the Dartmouth Swimming Club swam on Christmas morning in Castle Cove.

to poultry raising and a few other things of that sort for salvation. Poultry is bound to pay, our correspondents thinks, if managed on the same principle at the turkey that graced his board on Chsristmas Day. He was a fine bird but rather heavy for his size. An investigation of his interior explained the reason: for it brought to light the fact that the bird's natural weight had been increased by the addition to its contents of over a pound weight of small shot! The man who fed that turkey, says our correspondent, ought to read a paper on the raising of poultry before the Devon and Cornwall Chamber of Agriculture. He is a genius. Shots cost more than corn weight, no doubt, but then it lasts longer and when sold as dead turkey at a shilling a pound, it brings a clear profit of at least 100 per cent! The moral is so obvious that it needs no pointing.[72]

1894 'Under Stephen's Bow' by Iris

The following story was written by an author only identified as 'Iris' for *The Devon Weekly Times* in 1894. The unidentified house in the Pennsylvania district of Exeter was most likely similar to St German's Lodge or any of the other grand houses now part of the University of Exeter.

Under Stephen's Bow

A story of two Christmas Eves

Christmas Eve in the highways of Exeter and Christmas Eve in the byeways. A cold, biting, frosty evening; just the weather for Christmas everybody, who was warmly clad and well housed declared. Christmas Eve in the highways, and Christmas Eve in the byewsays. In one of those latter, just beyond, and under the shadow of that ancient arch called St Stephen's Bow, a slim, girlish figure was cowering over a dilapidated basket, the white blossoms in which she was re-arranging with slender, shapely fingers that trembled with the cold.

She sank wearily upon the flagstones when her task was ended, and for a moment leaned her throbbing forehead against the rough side of the arch, while a great, hopeless sob burst from her quivering lips. She was so poor, so hungry; and this was Christmas Eve. Some gay, happy folks who had just passed her had said so to each other in joyful tones, and, couching there in the shadow of Stephen's Bow, a wild prayer went up from the heart of the homeless wanderer, that she might never see the dawn of Christmas Day upon this cruel earth.

A fainting unconsciousness of cold and hunger, and the wares she ought to be selling, was stealing over the girl, when suddenly the face of a passer-by, tripping in her tattered gown, roused her and the young man, Jack Cameron, whose awkward haste (he had turned into Stephen Street as a near cut to an evening entertainment at a house in the Close) had caused him to almost tumble over the cowering figure he had not noticed in the semi-darkness, came to a full stop at once.

'I beg your pardon!', he said, and then, with a gentleman's instinct, seeing she was preparing to rise he held out his hand to assist her.

'It was my own fault', she murmured, in tones whose gentle refinement surprised and even startled him, 'I ought not to have been crouching there, but I was so weary, and it was a little sheltered from the wind'.

She was on her feet confronting him now, and, if he had been startled at her voice, he was still more so at sight of the picture she made in the light from a neighbouring shop window. There was a wonderful, almost unearthly, beauty to the small, oval face, and clear-cut features, framed by the curling, dark hair that escaped in rich profusion from under her battered, shabby hat; her figure was slight, and straight, and exquisitely, if unconsciously, graceful in its pose, as she stood, drooping like one of her own, frost-nipped flowerets, before him; and then the eyes – big, innocent eyes of deepest blue – that she raised to his, Jack Cameron could not recall their colour five minutes later, but he felt that the helpless, appealing look in their sorrowful depths had gone straight to his heart.

But the graceful form was shrouded in a cloak so worn and thin that the gleam of the little bare arm was visible through its texture, and as the young man noticed if he burst out in shocked tones.

'You poor child, to be abroad so lightly clad on such a bitter night. What are your friends thinking of? What is your name?'

'I am Elsa, sir!', she said, answering his last question first, 'and I have no friends.'

Then the business instinct that had been dormant a moment in sheer surprise at the handsome stranger's civility, awoke again in the little waif, and she picked up her basket of blossoms and held them to him, saying in eager tones.

'Please buy a flower, sir. See! They are Christmas roses, and beautiful, too.'

He began to say something, but checked himself, and, choosing three of the snowy blooms, he dropped half-a-crown into the basket.

'Have you no smaller change, sir?' she asked wistfully, 'I have none, and they are only a penny each.'

'That's alright. The flowers and my awkwardness together are not paid for with that,' he answered, as he strode hastily off down the gloomy pathway, and so, having turned his back upon her, he did not see the waif press the coin he had given passionately to her lips, before she consigned it to the bosom of her ragged dress, and hastened away in the opposite direction, with eyes shining through a mist of unshed tears that were not all of sorrow.

Half way across Cathedral Close Jack, whose hasty steps had become more and more undecided as he walked, came to a dead standstill.

'What can be the matter with me?' he thought. 'That girl's sweet, sad face is haunting me. A mere child like that – she can't be more than fifteen – to be alone and friendless in this busy city tonight. Homeless on Christmas Eve, that chit of a girl, while a big fellow like me has every comfort a human being can desire. I can't stand it. I'll go back and find her again. At least I can recommend her to a decent lodging, for old Nurse Penrhyn would take in anybody, and treat them well for my sake'.

He was retracing his steps as he made this resolve, and in a brief minute he stood again under the shadow of an arch, but the stream of light fell only on smooth

1894

At the West of England Eye Infirmary the Christmas dinner included roast turkey, boiled ham, plum pudding and fruit.

1895
Cases of bottles washed ashore at Teignmouth on Christmas morning.

flagstones and rugged wall; the little flower-girl was gone; and though he failed to keep his engagement, and spent the rest of the evening, and far into the night as well, in a fruitless walking up and down the busy streets, he saw the slight figure with its burden of white blossoms, that was already so indelibly impressed on his mental vision no more.

Jack Cameron had seen many a fair vision of girl hood in his time. Awful beauty had to put on all its charms many a time and oft for his especial benefits, for he was an only son, and heir to a very fair, unencumbered Devonshire estate, but not one of the Maries, and Noras, and Helens, whose charms assiduous female relations had enlarged upon so warmly, had touched his heart at all. Love was no ephemeral emotion with him, to be fallen into today and out of tomorrow, and so he could not understand the feeling that had possession of his soul through the days and weeks that followed; and it was only after the lapse of months, and that he found that that face and those eyes were as living realities to him still, as they had been when he had seen them for the first and last time under St Stephen's Bow, that he would acknowledge to himself that he, a gentleman born, and heir to broad lands, and a little more than the memory of a flower-girl, of whom he knew literally nothing but that she owned a sweet, flower-like face, innocent blue eyes, a gentle voice, and that her name was Elsa.

Eight years went by. Long enough for most men to forget even the wives they once swore to love and cherish, if those wives had ceased to exact the loving and cherishing; and it seemed as if the image that had filled Jack Cameron's mind once had grown blurred and indistinct there, for in the wide garden of one of the largest and pleasantest houses Pennsylvania boasted Jack was walking with slow and lingering steps by the side of a lovely girl, on the afternoon of another Christmas Eve.

They had strolled thus for some time, though Gracie Howard had been declaring for the last twenty minutes that each turn must be the last.

Presently one of the French windows of the drawing room was flung open by an impetuous hand, and a brisk, energetic little lady, who was well on past middle life, and who did not disdain to own it, by crowning her still dark and luxuriant hair with a dainty creation of lace and ribbon, called by courtesy a cap, came hastily across the lawn, with skirts carefully held up from contact with the crisp, frost-sparkling grass.

'Do you two want to catch your death of cold!' she called as she came near the couple. 'If you're not going to take better care of my Gracie than this is, Master Jack, I'm not at all sure that I shall give her to you on the twenty-third'.

'We were just coming in, Auntie,' the girl answered, while Jack apologised good-humouredly, and promised better behaviour for the future.

'Auntie', Grace began as they all three strolled back to the house in company, 'Jack wants to take me into the city to see the shops tonight. He says they are quite grand when they are lit up. You don't mind our leaving you, do you?'

'Mind, of course not, child.' But do you really wish to go, Gracie? I should have thought you had grown out of such childish folly. on Christmas Eve, too, dear', she added in a lowered voice.

Gracie stopped her remonstances with a hug, and directly their early tea was over, she tripped off to dress, and promptly joined her lover in the bright, well-lighted hall.

'Are you sure you will be warm enough Gracie?' he asked tenderly.

'Sir, you insult my furs,' she answered, smiling up at him out of their cosy depths and outside, when the hall door, and then the entrance gate, had clanged behind them, she went on.

'You may take my arm, if you will, though I generally dislike that way of walking; but it is very dark just here, and the asphalt is a trifle slippery.'

Exeter's main streets were as busy (and St Stephen's Bow as deserted) as they had been that Christmas Eve eight years before, and what with stopping to gaze into windows, in which recreation Gracie took as naive delight as a child, and being hindered by dodging the numberless groups of pedestrians passing hither and thither and every way, the lovers made their slow progress on their tour of inspection.

'Oh! Jack! Look! Christmas roses! And such beauties,' Grace said softly, pausing in front of a florist.

What could Jack do? What would any lover to but to respond to that appeal, and be grateful to his lady-love for permitting him to do so? So in a very few minutes Gracie was in the street once more, with both hands filled with the pure, snowy blooms, and the young man walking at her side, and gazing down at the slim, small figure, grew strangely and unwontedly quiet.

She noticed presently that he did not answer her merry chatter, and glancing up, was startled at the sombre, sorrowful look on his face.

'What is the matter Jack?' she asked. 'Have I offended you?'

'You couldn't do that, dear.' he said 'But– but, you and your Christmas roses had recalled something to my mind. I have a confession I ought to make to you, Gracie. Will you hear it now?'

'If you can tell me it in this crowded street,' she answered, in a low voice.

He slipped his hand under her arm, and walking so, unreproved for once, although it was in the public thoroughfare, he told her the history, slight and incomplete as it was, of that Christmas Eve that had had so much effect upon his life.

'She interrupted him abruptly as they reached the end of the pavement at Broadgate.

'Shall we turn here?' she said, and they retraced their steps.

'I am glad that I have told you, Gracie,' he concluded. 'A man should keep no past doings a secret from the woman he is about to make his wife. I am glad I have confessed to you that that little flower girl was my first love, and, if I could have discovered her, and had found her as good and innocent as she looked, she would

have been my last love. It is no disparagement to you to say so, is it, dear? I had not met you then.'

'No! No! Jack!' the girl answered, while her breath came quick through lips parted in suppressed excitement. 'I too,' she added, 'have a confession to make. Let us turn down here.' They were passing the end of St Stephen Street now. 'I can tell you best in the quiet bye-ways'.

She stepped a pace in front of him as they passed beneath St Stephen's Bow, and turning, stood in his path; and he, wondering at the action, stood still too and looked down upon her. As he did so, the light from the window fell full upon her face and figure, and her hands filled with the Christmas Roses, and in that instant, the past eight years vanished like a dream, and he saw that the fealty promised to Grace Howard, was no treason to the child who had won his heart by one look from her innocent eyes that Christmas Eve, for Gracie and the child were one and the same.

He knew, almost without hearing them, what the words were that parted those red lips now.

'I am Elsa, sir', she said.

A group of merry, noisy people was passing at the moment, and he resisted the impulse to clasp her to his heart, and only gave the hands he had taken, rose and all, in his own, a passionate pressure, and for a minute, each reading the soul in the other's eyes, neither of them spoke.

Reason asserted her away, however, presently, and Jack said, in bewildered tones.

'But I thought Miss Howard was your aunt, Gracie-Elsa'.

'And so she is; the dearest, truest kinswoman ever a girl had. I cannot collect my thoughts to tell you all now, Jack; besides, auntie knows the story so much better than I do. But that hour in which I met you eight years ago was the last of my life of privation and struggle. It seems Auntie had been seeking me for years; I am her dead brother's only child; and that evening she found me, she will tell you how, within thirty minutes of your leaving me. She made me call myself by my second name, Grace, to throw off as much as possible all memory of my former life. And I was so happy. And then you came, and I was happier still. I saw that you did not remember me. I did not expect you to. I did not think you could have given a second thought to the poor little waif whose good angel you seemed that Christmas Eve. But I knew you at once; a woman never forgets. And oh! Jack, it has been, since first you told me that you loved me, the fly in the ointment of my happiness, that I must some day tell you of my past, and so, perhaps, estrange you for ever. For, of course, I should not have suffered you to marry me in ignorance of the fact that I had once sold flowers in the street. And now, the cloud I so dreaded is breaking in greater showers of blessing than I have received before. Oh, it is too much happiness –'

'And what of my happiness, dearest?'
'Hush, Jack. Yours can be nothing compared with mine, for you have not known the horror of suspense – hark!' she broke off to say, with uplifted hand, listening to the carol the choir had just begun to practice in a church hard by.
'Peace on Earth – Good will to men.' You first taught me that such things existed, Jack, my Jack, eight years ago this Christmas Eve.'

1896
Fire broke out in a seedsman's shop in Totnes.

1895 Christmas Crackers of 1895

From: *The Devon Weekly Times.*

When is coffee like the earth?
When it is ground.

What's the difference between a French pastry-cook and a bill-poster?
One puffs up pastes and the other pastes up puffs.

Why should a man always run home with his wife's new bonnet?
To get there before the fashions change.

What will be the latest thing in bloomers?
The modest girl.

Why are troubles like babies?
Because they get bigger by nursing.

1897
Mr Harry Hems entertained 72 'broken-down citizens and their wives' at the 29th Annual Lucky Horseshoe Christmas dinner.

1898
The Seaton Christmas Pleasant Evening included a reading of Dicken's Marley's Ghost.

1895 Christmas at Chawleigh, Coleford and Washford Pyne

Three correspondents to *The Western Times* gave impressions of very different experiences over Christmas Week.

Chawleigh

The mummers, dressed in brilliant attire, visited the principal houses in the neighbourhood, and were well received.

Colebrooke

The villagers of Coleford have erected a lamp at the four crossways. It was lighted for the first time last week and illuminated the district all around. There is a story that one man came running into the village as he thought the place was on fire. The lamp is one of a hundred candle power and the youngsters celebrated its advent by dancing around it in high glee.

Washford Pyne

The diphtheria scare is over, but it has left a cruel gap in our ranks. We now know that pure water and cleanliness are absolutely necessary for health. If we have learnt that stagnant cesspools, impure wells and dirty habits mean disease, and probably death, the scourge has not visited us in vain. But have we all learnt it? Well, as the boy said when he spilt ink on the tablecloth, that remains to be seen.[73]

1895 'Pixie-led: A Christmas Adventure on Haldon'

The following story written by an anonymous writer was set on the road from Haldon Hill to Dartmoor.

I'm what they call a Moor Farmer, and if you know what that means, you won't expect any grand speechifying in a yarn from me; though my dear old missus, who came in from over the hill, and had a boarding school education in her youth, has promised to look over this when I've done and put it a bit ship-shape. She says that I must tell it myself.

It was a matter of twenty years ago it happened. Twenty years ago, to be precise, come Christmas Eve! First of all I ought to say that I, and my father before me, have farmed the estate, on the border of Dartmoor, where I'm living now, for more than three quarters of a century. Me and my missus are well nigh seventy years old; so you see we were about fifty that Christmas. The bit of a farm we live on, and one five miles away, are both our own, as well as a good bit of wild uncultivated ground where we run ponies, so you see we're a little rich in this world's goods, some of us moorland farmers.

But we were not rich in one way. We had no children. Two tiny mites had been given to us in the first four years of our married life, but they had both pined away, and died in infancy. It was the one crook in our lot, this lack of children's voices in our home.

All this has nothing to do with my story, you are thinking, but you will see.

I always make it a point to attend Christmas Market in Exeter, if I can. I don't go to Exeter I suppose more than half a dozen times in the year, but Christmas is always one of those times.

Well! Twenty years ago I'd had a bit of a cold the market-day, and my missus, she's a bit soft about me you know, and like to coddle me when I'll let her, had insisted that I must stay indoors for a day or two; so when it came to the morning of Christmas Eve, I couldn't realised that the next day would be Christmas Day, so says I:

'I think I'll go to Exeter to-day, old woman!'

'Well! John,' says she, 'If you do, there are a few little things I want, and you can bring them.'

So I started on my old brown cob, with a thick muffler about my neck, that I shoved into my pocket as soon as I was out of sight.

'John!' my missus called after me. 'Be sure to be home early to burn the ashen faggot.'

With her last words in my mind I had left Exeter before five o'clock on my return journey, and was jogging comfortably along the Alphington Road with every pocket of my coat bulging with parcels, and one or two tied on to the saddle. As far as Alphington Church I had company, but there my friend branched off to the right, and I followed the straight road.

In Kennford village I stopped at the Anchor for a glass. It was very dark by then, and the landlord wished my joy of my long, rough ride.

But I laughed at his sympathy till he said:

'It's just the night for the pixies to be abroad, you know.' I knew he was only laughing at the faith I shared with most of the old-world folks I'd been brought up amongst; which faith I hold still. I don't say the 'little people' are half so busy nowadays as they were when I was a boy. the railways, and telegraphs, and electric light, and the deuce knows what in the way of improvements, are enough to frighten them out of existence. But the pixies did some mighty queer things in my youth. Aye! and punished evil-doers, and rewarded the good, in a wonderful manner, too. Tell me the pixies never existed! How was it we always had to mark a cross on our heaps of newly-threshed corn else, but because they would have scattered it to the four winds, if we hadn't shown so that we knew who we had to thank for a plentiful harvest; see the men and women too, out of number, that I've known to be pixie-led in my youth. Old women going from work, who have had to wander, round and round a field, seeking the gate to go out, and passing it heaps of times, till the

1899

The sun shone at Totnes on Christmas Day.

1900

A wet Christmas at Starcross.

little people have chosen to cease their gaming, and let 'em go home. Last of all, haven't I been pixie-led myself? Wasn't I pixie-led that very Christmas Eve now twenty years ago? I'll tell you what happened after I left Kennford, and you can judge for yourself.

It's a quiet, dreary ride over Haldon at night, and apt to be dangerous sometimes, but I knew no fear, mounted on my stout nag, and with my heavy, lead-weighted hunting whip in my hand. I left the twinkling windows of a farm-house in the valley on the right, about a quarter of a mile from the village, behind me and after that I was going up Haldon Hill.

Old Brownie went so slowly, jogging from side to side on the wide road; perhaps, too, that last glass had made me somewhat sleepy; at all events I don't remember any more till my horse tripped over a loose stone, and almost pitching me over his head, awakened me into full possession of my faculties. (That's my old woman's sentence, not mine.) I sat upright in a moment, pulled Brownie up, and then became aware of two things at once – that I was on the top of Haldon and that I had lost my hat.

Where I'd lost it I didn't know. You see I didn't remember anything after passing the entrance to Trehill grounds, and it might have fallen off almost directly after I began to doze.

It was always a long enough journey for Brownie without doubling over any of the ground, and I, too, was anxious to get home, so I made up my mind to leave the hat where it was, tied a knot in each corner of my red handkerchief, pulled it on my head and well down over my ears, and started on again. Or thought I was going to; and that's where the little people come in. The minute I caught up the rein I could feel their presence, and I wasn't so terribly surprised when Brownie just set his four feet stiff, and refused to stir.

For why, sir? Why because the little people wouldn't let him go on. Tell me! The pixies knew what they were about that night, I always think that one of them may have knocked my hat off. anyway Brownie refused to stir, and when I have him a gentle reminder with the whip, he just turned square round, and began to trot back down the very road he had come up. I didn't try to stop him, because I knew for certain now it was the pixies' doing, and when at last he broke into a walk, I took that as a sign that I must get off and look for my hat; it must be about here I had lost it.

So down I got and with Brownie's bridle over my arm began to poke about among the brambles, and fallen leaves with the butt end of my hunting whip. Presently I struck something hard and round, and stooped to pick up the hat. Before I could rise again my blood was suddenly frozen in my veins by a strange, unexpected noise. Yet it was only the wildness of the place, and the hour that made the sound at all alarming, for it was the cry of a little child.

It came, it seemed to me, from close to my feet, and after the first start of surprise was over, I drew aside the brambles and plunged into the ditch that ran along the side of the road, looking quite eagerly for the origin (my missus again) of the sound, that was by this time increasing.

At last I stumbled on a market-basket, and, catching it up, was soon kneeling in the middle of the road, cutting the strings by which the cover was fastened down, with my clasp-knife. It was as dark as pitch just there, for the great trees on both sides of the road met overhead, and low enough down to make even a short man like myself look out for his head in riding under them, so when I'd got the basket open I had to fumble about to find matches, before I could see what my treasure trove was like.

It had ceased crying now, and when I held a lighted match over the basket I found that it was a fair little baby about a year old. Her dear little head, all a mass of glistening curls, were pillowed on some warm, red stuff, and she was tucked in cosily enough, and dressed up very warmly, we found later on.

Suddenly, as I looked at her lying there so quiet, and looking up at me without a bit of fright in her blue eyes, some half forgotten baldames yarns of long ago concerning pixie challenges flashed into my head, and a strange, uncanny fear made me wonder whether she were a human child at all, or if I had not better leave her where I had picked her up.

I know I couldn't have done so else, but, as if divining my thought she suddenly put up a tiny hand and grasped one of my big rough fingers as they rested on the edge of her basket, and stretched the other hand up to my face, with a little crow of delight.

She settled the matter then. I put the baby and hamper gently on quite old Brownie's back, jumped up carefully behind it, and so jogged home, Brownie going that way willing enough now. We rode into the farm-yard just as the kitchen clock struck twelve.

My missus was got very anxious, you may be sure, and perhaps the ferment she had been in about me made her receive the little burden I had brought home without a frown.

We advertised our find far and wide of course, but nobody sent to claim the child, though a few days after Christmas a letter came addressed to me in a strange writing, and when we opened it, there dropped out notes for £100 and a couple of lines.

'Take care of our darling, and bring her up as your own, and God will reward you.'

And we've done it, sir, and He has rewarded us, for she's been the sunshine of our home for twenty years. We've brought her up well, too, though I say it myself, and with her pianny, and her pretty French jabber, when she's a mind to it, she'd be no disgrace to her parents, whoever they are, though no one would claim her from us now, our pretty Noeline. That was the fine name my missus gave her, she said it was to do with her being found at Christmas time. But I – in compliment to the little people who guided me to her that night – I have never called her anything but 'Pixie'.[74]

1897 Christmas

An editorial in the *Exeter Flying Post*, simply entitled 'Christmas', mused on the holiday.

The eve of Christmas brings with it the welcome opportunity of relegating all disputative subjects to the limbo of temporary oblivion. For once in the year the privilege is available of treating a subject on which the unamity is wonderful, for it is a poor and a misanthropic that can discover anything to cavil at in this season of goodwill. The inception of Christmas as a period of social rejoicing is surrounded by a good deal of mystery. Christmas has not always been, as many people suppose, a purely religious festival. Indeed, when Christianity first began to spread beyond the neighbourhood of the Holy Land, there was no religious observance of the anniversary of the Nativity. Augustine himself, the first Archbishop of Canterbury, was of opinion that the observance had neither Apostolic origin or the sanction of a General Council, and when the question of observing the Advent was first considered there was much diversity of view as to the actual date, some contending, for the 20th of May, others for the 20th of April, others again for the 6th of January, several centuries elapsing before a general agreement was arrived at to fix the celebration for the 25th of December. Before the religious festival was introduced, however, the ancients were accustomed to indulge in various Pagan rites and rejoicings at the passing of the shortest day, and for a lengthy period Christmas was a curious combination of the Holy and the mundane. To this day those pre-Christian revelries survive in various forms – in the Yule log, the mistletoe, and the wassail bowl among others – adding picturesqueness to the telling of the most beautiful of all stories. Ascetics tell us that such survivals should be disassociated entirely from the religious festival, but many years of usage have in a manner sealed the conjunction. And we do not think that religion suffers thereby, for it is at this period that the finest traits of the Christian character are made manifest; it is now that harmony, peace, and concord dwell in the heart of every man and woman worthy of the name. To the English people the festival is especially dear, linked as to is with thoughts of those family ties which are the very head and front of the national life. It tends, if it does not actually lead, to a broadening and deepening of the mind, to the obliteration of self, and consequently to the development of the spirit of toleration and of friendship. Differences are forgotten, troubles are laid aside, and all meet on a common ground of decorous enjoyment which leaves the world much better than it was found. The religious influences elevate the tone of the festivities and impart a grace to the observance, leaving nothing for the self-appointed critics of mankind to cavil at. For about a generation now it has been our custom to greet our readers with the season's compliments. In the early days of newspapers the idea had not been born. Turning back to the files of the last century we find no message being sent forth to the reading world. We are glad to be enabled to partially repair this omission of our predecessors by expressing with double heartiness the wish that one and all of our readers may enjoy

A HAPPY CHRISTMAS AND A BRIGHT NEW YEAR.[75]

1897 A wish list for 1897

This Victorian list of children's presents would probably have appeared extraordinarily extravagant.

1901
The Hartland Chronicle *informed its readers that 'If a lamp is allowed to go out on Christmas Eve, it is an omen of death'.*

Tommy's Letter to Santa Claus

Dear Santa Claus, if you could bring
A patent doll to dance and sing,
A five-pound box of caramels,
A set of reins with silver bells;

An elephant that roars and walks,
A proper Punch droll that laughs and talks,
A humming-top that I can spin,
A desk to keep my treasures in;

A boat or two that I can sail,
A dog to bark and wag its tail,
A pair of little bantam chicks,
A chest of tools, a box of tricks;
A scarlet suit of soldier togs,
A spear and net for catching frogs
A bicycle and silver watch,
A pound or two of butterscotch;

A small toy farm with lots of trees,
A gun to load with beans and peas,
An organ and a music-box,
A double set of building blocks –

If you bring me these, I say,
Before the coming Christmas Day,
I sort of think, perhaps, that I'd
Be pretty nearly satisfied.[76]

1911
The newly-formed girl hand bell ringers in Appledore performed throughout Christmas.

1912
There were heavy storms over the holiday period: four vessels were driven ashore in Plymouth Sound, a gypsy tent in Holsworthy caught on fire and caused the deaths of two children, and on Boxing Day football supporters at Plymouth asked for their money back at half-time when a gale stopped the game from being played to a finish.

1897 Christmas Crackers

From *The Exeter Flying Post*:

Why is a temperance man sure not to sink?
Because he keeps his nose above water.

Why is it vulgar to sing and play by yourself?
Because it is so lo.

Why is the rudder of a steamboat like a public hangman?
Because it has a stern duty to perform.

Why are weary persons like carriage wheels?
Because they are tired.

What is always behind time?
The back of a watch.

What flower most resembles a bull's mouth?
A cowslip (cow's lip)

When has a man brown hands?
When he's tann'd em (tandem) driving.

Which eats more grass, black sheep or white?
(white, because there are more of them)[77]

1898 A Hartland social evening

By 1898 Christmas Social Evenings had established themselves in the north Devon village of Hartland. Most of those who attended wore costumes, not all of which would be socially acceptable today. A report in *The Hartland Chronicle* noted:

Social evenings with music, singing and dancing, are now considered quite the established order of things during Christmas Week. Two very successful socials were held in the Board Schoolroom on December 28 and 30. The company, which numbered about ninety on each evening, assembled at 7:30, many in fancy dress, which the committee made optional, and when dancing commenced, the room presented a very picturesque and animated scene. The following were some of the characters assumed on Wednesday, but several donned another costume for Friday.

1913
Robinson Crusoe *was Exeter's pantomime.*

Jockey:	H. Haynes
Knave of Clubs:	J.T. Haynes
Cyclist:	J.S. Haynes
Pierrot:	J. Hobling
Nigger:	J.D. Wilton
Dr Jim:	F. Wilton
Stars and Stripes:	H. Wilton
London Scottish:	T. Lyle
Nigger:	W. Jones
Cowboy:	Walker
Jester:	W. Walker
Page:	W. Pillman
Uncle Sam:	J. Haynes
Footman:	W. Bond
Yachtsman:	Griffiths
Sailor's lass:	Mrs Grenfell
Hospital nurse:	Mrs Hobling
Queen of Hearts:	Miss Lyle
Bo-Peep:	Misses Reynolds
Spanish:	C. Wilton
Japanese:	M. Wilton
Granny:	M. Chope
French fishwife:	M. Chope
Spanish Lady:	F. Walker
Swiss Peasant:	A. Haynes
Hindoo girl:	Prust
A bride:	M. Warder
Italian peasant:	Boswell
Gardeners' daughter:	Littlejohns
Christmas:	Burrow
Red Riding Hood:	Prouse
Housemaid:	Mrs Cann[78]

1900 A Clovelly Christmas Tree

In 1900 the first Christmas Tree was erected for the students of the Weslelyan Sunday School in Clovelly. *The Hartland Chronicle* reported that:

On Boxing Day a Christmas Tree (maintained due to the efforts of Mr Edwin Shackson) was given for the scholars of the Wesleyan Sunday School. A room kindly lent by Mr Shackson senior for the occasion was very gaily decorated with flags, etc. by Messrs Edwin Shackson and Tom Howard, who also attended to the decorations of the tree. At six o'clock the scholars and teachers, with others, assembled to receive, and witness the distribution of the presents. Christmas carols

1914
One hundred soldiers, some with frost bite, arrived in Exeter's hospitals in time for Christmas.

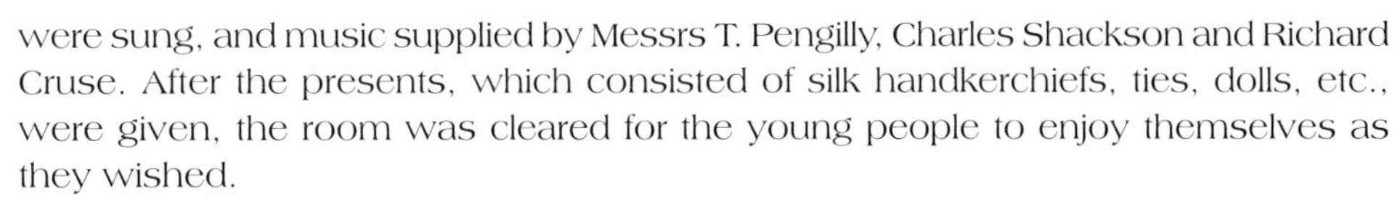
were sung, and music supplied by Messrs T. Pengilly, Charles Shackson and Richard Cruse. After the presents, which consisted of silk handkerchiefs, ties, dolls, etc., were given, the room was cleared for the young people to enjoy themselves as they wished.

Among those who helped to amuse the children were Mr T. Pengilly (superintendent), Captains Burnard, Jenn and Marshall, Messrs Shackson, Cruse and Howard, and the teachers and elder scholars of the Sunday School. All spent a most enjoyable evening. It is hoped as it proved such a success this year, that the Christmas tree will become an annual event.[79]

1903 A morning dip at Plymouth

The Western Weekly News reported a Christmas Swim in 1903 in a report entitled 'The Morning Dip, over 100 Bathers including ladies'.

There was a degree of sharpness in the air yesterday morning, too strong to be merely termed bracing. Nevertheless, that did not deter those who had signified their intention of bathing under Plymouth Hoe from taking a morning 'dip'. Between eight and nine o'clock about 100 men and boys, ages ranging from 15 to 60 and just over, assembled on the rocks near the Promenade Pier, and whilst many sought the shelter of the bathing-houses, a large number – perhaps the majority, went to the full extreme, and undressing on the rocks, plunged into the cold-looking sea. The sun shone on the bathers, but it was an 'Arctic sun' and gave very little comfort. The morning was without doubt cold; but it seemed as though many of the bathers had to partake of their morning dip before becoming cognisant of the fact. Mingling among the crowd on the rocks, it was an easy matter to select those who had bathed from the non-venturesome. There was remarkably little fussiness among those who had signified their intention of bathing that they might participate in a prize distribution customary on that occasion. A short dive and a short swim was the rule, and the exception, a dive from the highest part of the Promenade Pier by Mr S.G. Merryfield. Some amusement was caused by two elderly men swimming out some distance with a dog, and returning to the shore floating, the animal towing them, the foremost of the two men holding the dog by the tail. Two or three families were represented by three bathers. No fewer than 79 bathers assembled on the Promenade Pier for the prize distribution, local tradesmen having been very generous to the committee, Messrs. W.H. and J.H. Irish and E.A. Conybear. From the ladies bathing-place a few ladies bathed, two having quite a long swim. Nine of the men who bathed and took prizes were dumb.[80]

1903 A prehistoric Christmas

The following appeared in *The Western Weekly News.*

1. The pre-historic Christmas party kisses the pre-historic goose under the mistletoe, ensuing jealousy of the pre-historic turkey.

2. The pre-historic Christmas turkey cries "Ha, ha, a time will come,–!"

1915
Wet weather throughout Devon in Christmas Week.

1916
Owing to a shortage of labour, work came to a standstill at Castle Drogo.

1917
Babes in the Wood *played on Christmas Day at the Riviera Cinema, Teignmouth.*

1918
Three former German prisoners of war returned home to Teignmouth in time for Christmas.

1920
Two days before Christmas the snow began to melt at Salcombe after falling ten days before.

1921
Chagford beat Moretonhampstead at football on Boxing Day.

1923
Gypsies selling holly and mistletoe disrupted Newton Abbot's Christmas Market through fighting.

1925
Five foot drifts of snow were reported in north Devon over Christmas.

1928
HMS Devonshire *was nearing completion at Devonport.*

3. Enter the pre-historic Christmas turkey accompanied by the fearsome snapdragon.

4. The good Christmas fairy (of far-away times) turns the pre-historic turkey into cold turkey for supper.

1911 Christmas gifts

1911. CHRISTMAS PRESENTS. 1911.

COSIES,	TABLE CENTRES,	CUSHIONS,
HANDKERCHIEFS,	SACHETS,	HANDKERCHIEF BOXES,
PINAFORES,	GLOVES,	APRONS,
TRAY CLOTHS.	FANCY LINENS.	UMBRELLAS.

TO BE OBTAINED AT

MELTON'S, 38, High Street, TOTNES.

GRAMAPHONES! GRAMAPHONES!

Special Offers for Xmas Trade

AT

JORDAN'S, 94, High St., Totnes.

Splendid Tone Gramaphone, WITH LARGE HORN. AND TEN GRAMAPHONE SELECTIONS, £1 12 6

Larger Size, Ditto, - £2 2 0

Local Agency for "HIS MASTER'S VOICE" Gramaph ones. Choice selection of new records. Call and hear the Records made by Caruso, Melba, Clara Butt, and leading artistes of the day.

OF TOYS & FANCY GOODS

Our stock is larger and better than ever.

MECHANICAL TOYS, WORKING MODELS, XMAS CARDS,

And Useful Articles of all descriptions.

H. MATTHEWS & SONS', Ltd.,

Delicious Christmas

PLUM PUDDINGS

Should now be posted to friends abroad.

COST INCLUDING POSTAGE.

	2lb	3lb	4lb	6lb	8lb
ADEN, BARBADOS, BURMAH, BERMUDA, BRITISH EAST AFRICA, BRITISH HONDURAS, CHINA, HONG-KONG, CYPRUS, CANADA, GIBRALTAR, GOLD COAST COLONY, INDIA, JAMAICA, LAGOS, AFRICA, MALTA, NEWFOUNDLAND, NEW ZEALAND	3/-	5/-	6/-	8/-	9/8
NIGERIA, SOMALILAND (BRITISH), STRAITS SETTLEMENTS, SIERRA LEONE, WEST INDIES	3/-	5/-	6/-	8/-	9/8
ZANZIBAR, EGYPT	3/	4/9	5/9	7/6	9/2
CAPE COLONY, NATAL, ZULULAND, TRANSVAAL, ORANGE RIVER COLONY	4/3	6/-	7/9	11/-	14/3
AUSTRALIA, TASMANIA	4/-	5/6	7/-	9/6	12/2

CASH MUST ACCOMPANY ALL ORDERS.

11 & 12, Bedford Street, PLYMOUTH.

A. TARRING, BAKER & CONFECTIONER, 70, High Street, TOTNES,

Desires to inform his Customers that he will have his usual supply of

CHRISTMAS CAKES.

Your Orders Solicited.

MINCE PIES AND MINCE MEAT, CHOCOLATES AND FANCY CONFECTIONERY IN GREAT VARIETY. COSAQUES, CRACKERS, ETC.

MAKER OF MUFFINS & CRUMPETS.

Awarded Two Second Prizes for White Bread (London).

G. CANN, Baker, Cook & Confectioner,

Nealy Opposite the Market, 33, High Street, Totnes.

Desires to inform his Customers that Orders for

CHRISTMAS and OTHER CAKES

Will be promptly Executed. Excellence of Quality.

CHRISTMAS PLUM PUDDINGS, MINCE PIES, TARTS and FANCY PASTRY are made daily. Sole Agent for Bermaline Bread. A good Assortment of Bon-Bons, Crackers, Chocolates in Fancy Boxes, and Confectionery of kinds. Early Orders Solicited.

☛ QUALITY IS OUR TRADE MOTTO.

W. A. WARWICK & SON, 22, HIGH ST., TOTNES.

Confectioners and Caterers.

Christmas Specialities. Mince Meat. Plum Pudding. Rich & Plain Cakes of all Kinds.

Seasonable Supper Dishes prepared to order. Boned Turkeys. Boned Fowls. Game Pies, Veal and Ham Pies. Cooked Tongues and Hams.

Cream, Jellies and all kinds of Fancy Sweets :—: Sole Agents for Fuller's Confections.

QUALITY IS OUR TRADE MOTTO. ☚

CHRISTMAS 1911.

B. MARKS, Baker and Confectioner,

5, FORE STREET, TOTNES,

Desires to announce that he will have a good supply of

CHRISTMAS CAKES.

FANCY CAKES of all kinds, MINCE PIES, CHOCOLATES & FANCY CONFECTIONERY

Early orders respectfully solicited.

Christmas and New Year Presents.

Show Rooms now Open

AT

S. J. VEASEY'S

12, HIGH STREET, TOTNES,

With a Choice Selection of

CHRISTMAS AND NEW YEAR CARDS,

DOLLS, TOYS, GAMES,

And a Variety of Fancy Goods to suit all.

Note the Address: 12, High Street, TOTNES.

1929
A new white altar was dedicated at Alfington.

1930
420 parcels were given out to the poor of Bideford.

1931
A snowball whist drive was held in Halberton.

1932
Rabbiting parties took place in Talaton's farms.

1911 Devonport warships and Torquay hospitals

Christmas in 1911 was very different in Devonport and Torquay from those a few years later during the first world war.

Devonport

Probably never before in the history of Devonport have so many warships given Christmas leave in the port. The local sub-division of the Home fleet, with destroyers and tenders, has now reached the proportions of a very respectable fleet, and in addition there are in the port half a dozen fully-commissioned vessels namely the battleships *Bellephron*, *Collingwood*, *Temeraire*, and *Vanguard*, and the cruisers *Indefatigable* and *Gloucester*. Of the Second Division there are in the port the battleship *Colossus* and the cruiser *Bristol*, while the Atlantic fleet is represented by the battleship *Queen* and the cruiser *Dartmouth*; and among other ships *Cornwall* and *Cumberland*. Altogether there were in the port over a hundred warships, representing practically every type of fighting vessel afloat from the modern Dreadnoughts to the smallest submarine; and for every ship in this great fleet the King's Harbourmaster (Captain Le Marchant) was able to provide in the Hamoaze, so that officers and men were able to pass between their ships and the shore with a minimum of difficulty and danger in any weather. Generous leave had been given, and wherever possible the arrangements enabled one watch to spend Christmas Day in their homes and the other watch to be with their friends. Short leave was also granted to as many men as could be spared, so that in some of the vessels, especially those carrying only nucleus crews, the numbers remaining on board was comparatively small. But everywhere there was evidence of a splendid spirit of comradeship and of a determination to spend the day happily. In some cases there was hardly a touch of 'Christmas' to be seen at 7 am, but so completely had been the preparations that within an hour or two bunches of holly had been fixed to the mastheads, and main decks had become ablaze with decorations. A lower-deck 'poet' in one of the ships in basin was responsible for the following lines, which were pinned at the end of his mess

> A merry Christmas to you all.
> So let us then begin;
> The ship is very wet without,
> And very dry within.

But after 'eight bells' at any rate, there was an abundance of 'good cheer' in every ship; and every man on board had as much as he liked to eat, and as much to drink as was good for him. After dinner the men spend the day according to their own sweet will, and as spiteful, driving showers alternated with brief intervals of sunshine, it was no hardship to pass the day on board.

Torquay

At the entrance to the Torbay Hospital there was a pretty display of decoration with flags, trailing ivy, and Japanese lanterns. The various wards were also brightly adorned with seasonable mottoes, and tastefully draped by the sisters and nurses, under the direction of the matron, Miss Viola Billing. The Coronation Ward was decorated in red, white and blue; and a representation of a Japanese garden was very interesting. In the children's ward there was a remarkably realistic representation of the seaside with sand, boats, refreshment and bathing tents, and other attractions; and the little patients looked very pleased as they sat up in bed and played with their Christmas presents. At the entrance to the Florence Nightingale Ward there was a charming representation of 'the lady with the lamp' and in the ward itself were two large bell-shaped aquariums containing goldfish. At 5 am carols were sung by the nurses in the various wards.

At the Mildmay Home for Consumptives the nine patients were awakened by the singing of carols. Those who were able came down to breakfast, and received various presents, and the wards were prettily decorated. Dinner consisted of turkey and plum pudding. Later in the day an entertainment, consisting of a dialogue and songs, was given by the staff. Christmas gifts were sent by kind friends of the home.[81]

1933
Beef was more expensive than in previous years.

1934
The Town Band serenaded Hatherleigh on Christmas Eve.

1935
Heavy rain flooded the rivers Clyst, Otter, Axe and Yarty on Boxing Night.

1936
On Boxing Day Gracie Fields featured in Queen of Hearts *at The Cinema, Holsworthy.*

1913 Christmas Crackers of 1913

From *The Exeter Flying Post*:

Why are pretty girls like fireworks?
Because they soon go off.

Why is a pretty woman like a lock?
Because she is a thing to a door.

Why is a plum cake like the ocean?
Because it contains many currants.

Why is a cautious man like a pin?
Because his head prevents him from going too far.

Why is a fast young lady like a steamboat?
Because she never goes ahead without drawing a swell after her.[82]

1937
Barnstaple's Hawley Sanatorium was floodlit.

1938
Hand bell ringers toured the village of Poltimore on Christmas Eve.

1939
Two babies were born in Plymouth on Christmas, one was named Noel.

1940
Jack in the Beanstalk *was Exeter's pantomime.*

1914 The American Santa Claus ship at Plymouth

In early December of 1914 an American ship arrived at Plymouth with children's presents. After delivering its cargo the ship sailed to the continent on its voyage of good will.

The American Santa Claus ship *Jason* dropped anchor on Wednesday morning in Plymouth Sound. She was met at the Eddystone by a destroyer flotilla, and cordial greetings were exchanged.

The *Jason*, which belongs to the United States Government, has brought over a shipload of gifts for the children of the belligerent nations. Her cargo consists of warm clothing of every king, toys, and many other things to cheer the innocent sufferers from the horrors of war. Over 200 newspapers in America have assisted in the project. The *Jason* was berthed at Devonport later in the day, when Earl Beauchamp and Mr Acland were present on behalf of the British Government to receive the consignment for England. Plymouth gave the *Jason* a cordial welcome, the town being decorated and all the ships in the harbour dressed. The Jason's next port is Marseilles, where she will disembark the presents for the French, and then she will meet the United States battleship *Carolina*. The presents for Germany and Russia will be afterwards delivered. Belgium's quota will be landed at Plymouth.[83]

1923 The South Devon earthquake

The Western Times reported an earthquake happening in Devon on Christmas Day in 1923:

Apparently south Devon experienced a slight shock of earthquake on Christmas night over a wide area. Experiences differ considerably but all are agreed that there was a distinct tremor which shook houses, set crockery vibrating and in the country led to the belief that farm buildings were collapsing, while it alarmed the poultry. It was noticed at South Brent, Rattery, Diptford, Harberton, Harbertonford and Totnes.

Many speak of hearing something like a terrific bang, like that of an explosion and rumbling noises.

'We thought at first, ' said a lady, 'that it was heavy thunder but it was something different. The floor shook with a funny vibration as if there were something underneath it'.[84]

1923 Memories of Christmas in Victorian Hartland

In 1923 Mr Richard Pearse Chope recorded his memories of his childhood Christmas. He lived in the north Devon village of Hartland.

... I must pass on to Christmas, the most interesting period of the year, for, from Christmas Eve to what was formerly Old Christmas Day (January 5th) – it is now two days later – there was a continuous round of enjoyment and merriment. In preparation for Christmas Eve the great kitchen was decked with evergreens – chiefly holly and laurel – and from the centre of the ceiling was hung a 'kissing bush' – not formed of mistletoe, for that was unknown to us – 'the mistletoe doesn't grow where the nightingale doesn't sing' – but consisting of a small bush of *uuz* (furse), which was damped, sprinkled with flour and studded with holly berries. A few rosy apples were suspended immediately beneath it just out of reach, and any person was allowed to jump up and bite at them. The floor, made of Dinniball (Delabole) slate slabs, was, of course, washed and sprinkled with sand, and all round by the walls was scored with patterns made with Bath brick. I can imagine no more cheery-looking place for Christmas festivities – the large open hearth with a roaring fire, the curved oak settle on one side of it, the dresser shining with pewter and *cloam* (earthenware) immediately opposite, the grandfather's clock with its brass ornaments at one side, and the *clavy-tack* (mantelpiece) with its polished brass candlesticks, pestle and mortar, and various *joanies* (earthenware figures) – all of which are described in Mr Laycock's article.

This was the day for burning the *ashen fackit* (ash faggot) in commemoration of our Saviour's birth. It is said that he was first washed and dressed by a fire of ash wood, which ever since can be burnt when green. But the origin of the *ashen fackit* is more probably the Yule log of our forefathers, from which a fire can be raised by the aid of a pair of bellows, at any moment, day or night, in token of the ancient custom of open hospitality at such a season. The *fackit* consisted of a large log of ash in the middle, surrounded by smaller branches which were bound to it by a number *beens* (bands) – generally nine – of withy or *hales* (hazel). This filled the whole hearth, and it was lighted from the remains of the log of the previous year, which had been kept smouldering for the whole twelve days of Christmas. All the family, visitors, farm hands, and servants sat round it in a semicircle and watched it burning. As each band burst, a quart of cider was 'craved' and drunk out of small *hornen* drinking cups, and there was much shouting and hilarity, singing of songs, and cracking of jokes, until all the bands had burst. This pleasing custom has nearly died out, on account of the substitution of the *bodley* for the open hearth, but, as recently as 1878, Mr P.F.S. Amery found that it was kept up at 32 farms and cottages in the Ashburton postal district alone.

The party generally dispersed about midnight, but, before many hours had passed, the sleepers were disturbed by the waits singing their Christmas carols. With us the waits were all members of the Church choir, including men, women and boys, and many a weary trudge they must have had over heavy country roads, often covered with snow, in their wanderings from farmhouse to farmhouse. They usually reached us in the early morning – between 4 and 6 o'clock, I think. We were always roused out of our sleep to hear them, but were not allowed downstairs. The singers were invited into the house for refreshments and donations; the normal drink on the occasion being lamb's wool, hot spiced cider with roasted apples and toast floating in it. In this, of course, was drunk the health of the master and his family, with wishes for a merry Christmas. Next day to Church, to sing with what voices they had left.

The day after Christmas Day – 'the feast of Stephen' – was then, as now, a general holiday. The chief diversions were ferreting and rabbit-shooting, and, I think, badger-hunting, but I am afraid many still crueller sports were carried on. One of these was 'sparrow-mumbling' or 'muzzling the sparrow': a boy had his hands tied behind him, and the tip of one wing of a sparrow or other small bird placed between his teeth; he then tried, by the action of his teeth and lips alone, to draw the wing into his mouth and bite off the bird's head, the bird in the meantime pecking at his cheeks and eyes, and making frantic endeavours to escape. Whether this custom had any connection with 'hunting the wren' as performed in the Isle of Man and elsewhere, I am unable to say. Another curious game, or rather trick, called 'catching the owl' was practised at this or any other season, on raw farm hands. The lad was directed to stand beneath the tallet opening, holding a sieve over his head, and to watch for the owl while his companions went aloft to drive it out. Instead of this, they poured down a bucketful of filthy liquid into the sieve and drenched the poor lad from head to foot. Not many years ago I was told by a man that he had been caught by this trick when he was a farm lad.

The evening of St Stephen's Day was a favourite time for having the 'Harvest Feast' but different days, varying from Christmas Eve to Old Christmas Day. Everyone who had helped in the previous harvest, and, as several of the voluntary helpers had worked on different farms, they often got more than one invitation. A fine time they had. First of all there was a dinner or supper such as they rarely tasted – a huge round of beef, suet pudding, plenty of vegetables and a Christmas pudding – and as much cider or beer as they could drink. Then followed songs, games, cards, dancing, and such like. Generally the sole instrument of music in my younger days was a concertina, but, in earlier times, some of the church instruments, I believe were occasionally used, and even the *humstrum*, a sort of zither. The songs did not come without a lot of persuasion, but, when the good liquor had lubricated the men's tongues, they followed each other freely. The songs were very mixed – old and new – but such old songs as 'Jan Barleycorn' and 'When Joan's ale was new' were always favourites. The dances were hearty but peculiar – dancing over a broomstick, the sailor's hornpike, country dances, Sir Roger, and such like. As many as 20 or 30 persons used to take part.

The next evening the labourers' children were generally entertained in a similar but simpler fashion. After a good tea, they played various games, such as 'turn the trencher' or 'forfeits', blind man's buff and various kissing games, and they often had a magic lantern or shadow play provided for them.

The farmers' children also had their parties. About eight or ten of the chief farmers in the parish used to have a series of parties in turn, at which 20 or 30 children would be present, and, as these parties went on night after night, and lasted from

5 o'clock till midnight, and often till 1 or 2 in the morning, with a drive in an open trap for four or five miles afterwards, you can imagine the condition of the children at the end of their dissipation. I often wonder how we survived!

I shall not say much about the mummers, for I never saw them. Bands of young men, with masks or blackened faces and fancy garments, still go about from farmhouse to farmhouse, but I am told they no longer perform the old Christmas play of St George.

New Year's Eve is another date, for love-charms and divination, and New Year's Day also has its omens. You should open the door to let the New Year in; if the first person you see is a woman or a dark person, you will be unlucky, but if a man or a fair person, you will have good luck during the year. I don't know what happens if the woman happens to be fair, or the man to be dark. If a person, whose name (I don't know whether it is Christian name or surname) begins with a T, enters the house before noon, trouble will follow; and if the person who enters has the dreaded initial F, there will be a funeral from the house before another years comes round. If you sweep dust out of the front door, or throw away water, on that day, your luck will go with it. It is very unlucky, too, to wash clothes on that day.

The moon has a very potent influence in folk beliefs, and especially in love charms and divination. Thus, on the evening of the first full moon after New Year's Day, girls go out and stand on the spars of a gate or stile, and, looking up to the moon, say: –

All hail to thee, moon, all hail to thee!
I prythee, good moon, reveal to me
This night who my husband will be.

Then she bows low to the moon, goes to bed directly, and dreams of her future partner. Such operations as killing pigs, curing herrings, making cider and brewing should never be performed when the moon is *bating* (waning), for meat will not then take salt and cannot be cured, and new fermented liquors turn sour ...[85]

1941

A party was held in Gittisham for the evacuee children from London.

1942

The Victory Club, a group of Payhembury girls, sang carols to buy a life-saving jacket for the navy.

1943

Tyrone Power featured in Son of Fury *at The Cinema, Holsworthy on Boxing Day.*

1925 Christmas gifts

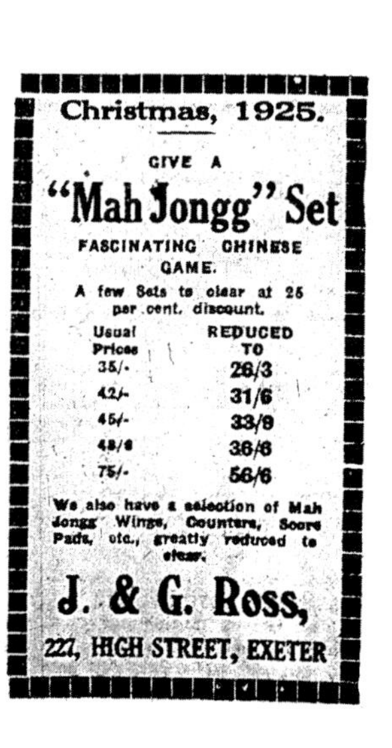

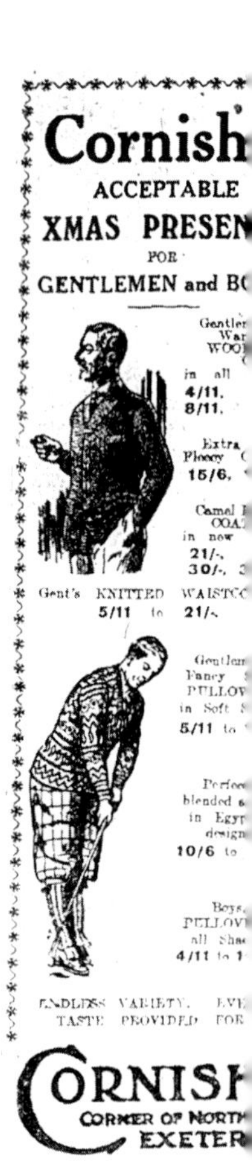

1944
Thick fog throughout Devon in Christmas Week.

1945
A jumble sale in aid of the Welcome Home Fund took place in Hartland a week before Christmas.

1946
Food shortages hindered providing traditional Christmas meals.

1937 Christmas gifts

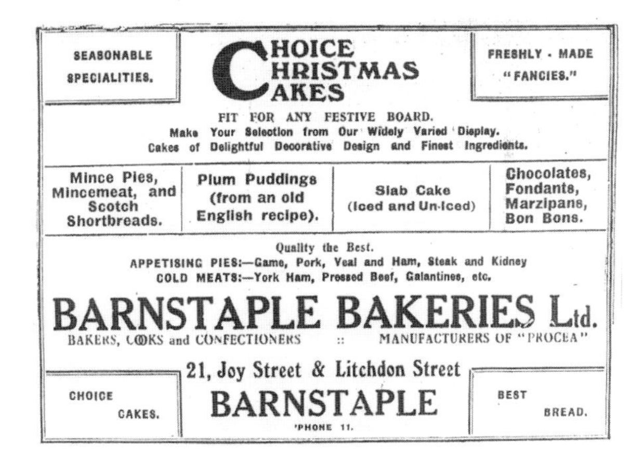

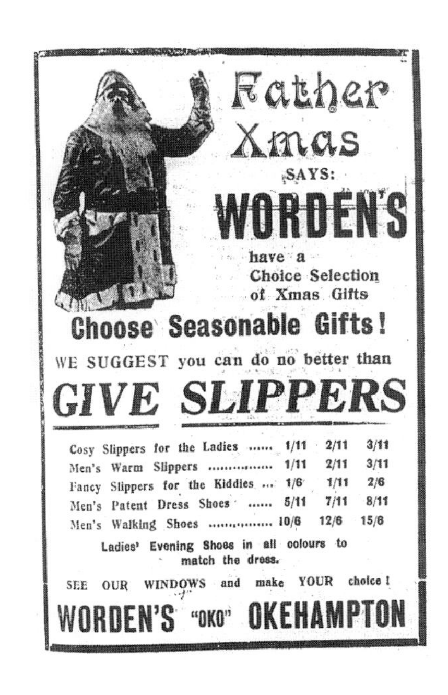

1942 Christmas Eve in Exeter Cathedral

The following story was written by I.M. Truman in the year that the city of Exeter was bombed in the second world war.

I cannot tell you how lovely it was in the Cathedral. It was all a beautiful dim, warm glow, but you could not see where it came from. You might have thought it was the lights on the Christmas tree, but they had all been turned out hours ago, at sundown, when the Cathedral was locked up. Who could be there at this time of night and what could they be doing?

Of course, it might be the firewatchers. Yet there was no sound of footsteps, no voices, however low; moreover, the Cathedral itself seemed to be different, it did not seem to be the hurt Cathedral that we have got used to lately: it seemed to be the old Cathedral just as it used to be, as it was last Christmas, as if, for this one night at least, its hurts had been healed.

There was a sound, though. There was a faint hush-hush, as of dozens of birds' wings; and there was a hint too of music in the air, as though minstrels tuned their instruments. There was above all, an unmistakable thrill, a thrill of expectancy and hope, a glow, not only of light, but of feeling, an urgent stir, as of countless living creatures, for the moment held in leash, awaiting life and freedom.

Now I don't pretend to know how those two singing boys got into the Cathedral at that time of night, but there they, and for some purpose too, for they were standing in the dim sanctuary, habited in alb and amice, and each bore a lighted taper, slender and waxen, in his hand. It flickered oddly through the arches, and sent unexpected lights and shadows up into the galleries and clerestory, so that you would have said there was some movement there, some sort of procession. But that could not be.

But the more you looked the more you thought you saw something moving, anything moving, everything moving. The boys stood waiting, motionless; but from everywhere else there was a continuous, streaming movement. This came from every direction, it seemed endless and ceaseless; what could it be?

The city clocks struck 11, and slowly the light increased. A vast procession was just beginning to form.

At the centre of it all was a Bishop, a tall, erect, rather imperious looking figure with the air of one who led, and who expected to be followed. Before him stood ready – surely not; – but it was so – the Angel minstrels from the minstrel gallery with their instruments which they held ready tuned (that was the faint music, then) to begin at the right moment. After them came our Lady's Tumbler, and the company of Cathedral Fiddlers; and then a host of Kings and Queens, Bishops and Dignitaries, Knights and Ladies, and all the folk who lie carven in stone, come to do honour to this Holy Eve. But besides these waiting figures, what is this moving concourse? Every animal in the Cathedral has been set free, and is joining in a wonderful streaming movement from all parts of the building, part on the ground but far the larger part winding along the galleries in the walls, getting longer and longer as it goes, and coming down all the little staircases out through the narrow little doors into the Nave and Choir to take their part and place among those who were waiting even now for their coming. We can recognize Roger's dog, of course, the reading monkey, the griffins, the pelicans, the elephants, the two-headed creatures looking rather awkward, sometimes in their eagerness pulling in two directions at once; the swans, who must have been thankful to straighten their poor cramped necks through their chains, still clanked rather heavily on them. Still there they were, with head straight up, and their bills moving gently as if they were whispering to themselves the words of the Benedict, 'O all ye birds of the Lord, praise y the Lord'.

There were the smiling dragons with their beautiful wings half spread, (Praise the Lord, ye dragons); a whole herd of boars, the wolf with the leaf in his mouth showing he was a converted wolf who had renounced his evil ways and become a vegetarian; Roger the Cementarius or Mason, was there himself, in the midst of them, with Walter the Verrour the Glazier, standing by one of the little doors with his horn, to welcome those who were coming down from the galleries, and marshal in their sudden liberty to their due place in the procession, lest their joy should break all bounds. Round these two were gathered all the faithful little hounds that have lain so long at the feet of their masters, without so much as a twitch of the whiskers or a wag of the tail. They wagged them now, in fact their whole bodies wagged, from the tips of their tails to their sniffing noses.

Even the snail was there, though as he was rather slow, all he could do from his place in the Children's Chapel was to reach the gate. It took him all the time the procession was going round to do even that bit, but as it got him exactly the right spot, it seems as if slowness does not matter if you get there. As it was it got him to the best place of all, right at the front.

The mermaids and the fishes were helpless, poor things, they had to stay where they were. But they flourished their tails.

Now I haven't told you half of the things that were moving. It was like the Benedicite in life and being. If you wanted to know them, you would have to spend hours and days in the Cathedral before you got acquainted with them. There were quiet nun-like women, stern-faced old monks, there was the man whose toothache has bothered him for so long; tonight he has lost even the memory of it. He has to hold his poor aching face for 364 days but tonight his hands are freed and he is waving them over his head. His smile was lovely. Everyone knows what it is to lose a toothache. There was a certain Bishop smiling kindly at a Canon – or was it an Archdeacon? Who could not smile back easily because his mouth was stiff from having to keep it open for so many years, and it was so nice to be able to shut for an hour or two. He looked up at the Bishop very politely now and then, and they seemed to have sort of understanding together, as if something regrettable had happened in the past, but that now they could afford to treat it as a joke.

There were squirrels who could not proceed slowly for they seemed to have all the joy of Christmas in their little pews, and they sprang from arch to arch, slid down the pillars, leapt on to the pulpit and lectern, along the tops of the choir stall canopies and swarmed over the screen to reach the corner in their own way. It was lovely to see them all free, all dancing with joy and life.

By this time you could begin to see some order in it all. The procession began up through the Choir, where the Dog Whipper, clothed in his gown and with his silver tipped wand of office, has led them, and where we lose sight of them for the moment.

The Angel Minstrels followed after, and after that again the Bishop, followed by the great congregation. Rank and place vanish when the Cathedral comes alive, for there is only one here tonight who is of Royal Rank, and we are brethren. Up they went, Kings and Queens, nuns and monks, great lords and beggars, dames and masons, organists and crusaders, the Crimean soldiers, the Knight and his cripple, the little lady with lute and her piper; the young girls, the saints and the children; and then all that wonderful collection of living creatures from all their positions on walls and arches, corbels and chantries, tombs and screening and vaulted roof.

The Dog Whipper has led the way all round the Choir and has come down the south side of the Cathedral to the West and is leading the way up the centre. The stately line of Angel Minstrels is there, with their strange looking instruments – the citrole, the bagpipes, the recorder and the viol; the harp and the Jews' harp; the trumpet and the organ; the gittern and the shawm; the timbrel and the cymbals. The Bishop came then, beautiful in gleaming white cloth of gold; then the massed people, then the amazing unending line of animals. Right at the end came the Sow and her litter. She had had such difficulty in keeping them together all round the Cathedral. 'Just in time, just in time', she muttered, her lean sides shaking with hurry. 'Oh all ye beasts and cattle, bless ye the Lord. Come children'.

The Bishop turned to the North Transept and lo, it was transformed. The whole place was as a poor stable, all else was gone. All the Angels who live in the Cathedral were gathered there, rank on rank, all round the walls and now you saw whence light came. It was the glow from them. In the centre of the space was a low pent roof with deep eaves, and beneath it two figures, the one the young slight maiden with the Babe in her arms that you can see on the corbel, the other, the tall guardian Joseph. The manger was empty. The ox and ass were encased in queer, basket-like stalls as you can see for yourself if you know where to look.

Between the Angels' wings, now and then, you could catch a glimpse of fields. Overhead, in the darkness, hung a star …

Now as the Bishop arrived it still wanted a few minutes to midnight, and suddenly the soft rushing sound that had been going on all the time became louder and clearer. Another Bishop, glorious in robes and mitre (a similar figure) came from the south aisle right into the centre of the concourse. He held out his arms, and behold, fifty four little owls came floating down from where they had been flying, and covered the Bishop and the Crib perching on every available place, on his hands and arms and shoulders, on the stable floor, manger and roof. Everything seemed covered with their soft downy bodies.

A third Bishop, with tall acolytes bearing tapers, came down the stair from the screen above. All was now ready, hushed and waiting.

The Maiden stopped, laid her Babe in the manger, and the Clock began to strike midnight.

Two streaks of shadows slipped through the cloister door, shot across the Cathedral, raced round and thrust through and between the massed figures until they were close to the front with Bishop Oldham and the owls, as close to the Manger as they could get. Of course one was Tom the Cathedral cat, and the other his beautiful friend, an exquisite creature gleaming like pale gold in the shadowed light.

As the clock struck, left by the three Bishops, every creature in that vast assemblage bent the knee.

There was a breathless hush. Then the two Singing Boys lifted their tapers, and the whole Choir blazed with light, though there was no visible light except those two tiny flames. Bishop Grandisson – yes, of course, we can see that now, it is he who is leading it all – sang with the two boys the words that you are so familiar with and the whole assembly, accompanied by the minstrels, sang the reply.

> 'Today the King of Heaven hath deigned to be born
> of a pure Virgin,
> That He might restore lost mankind.
> The Angelic Host rejoiceth for that eternal salvation
> Hath appeared to the children of men.'

Two tall Angels, accompanied by six more Singing Boys, came down from within the Choir and, with the other two, stood at the Golden Gates, to hand on the glad tidings to a world at war. As they sang the glow increased until the whole Cathedral was a blaze of heavenly light and beauty.

'Glory to God in the Highest' they sang, 'peace on earth to men of good will. Alleluia'.

'Glory to God in the Highest' sang the Cathedral Angels then, gathered in the North Transept. 'And on earth peace to men of good will. Today the Lord hath shone upon us. Alleluia, Alleluia, Alleluia.'

'Alleluia, Alleluia, Alleluia,' sang the hidden choristers of all the ages, massed behind the screen in the Choir.

'Alleluia, Alleluia, Alleluia,' sang the strange congregation, completing the threefold act of worship.

'Tuwhit, tu – whoo – oo', murmured the little owls, nestling out into a great soft bank, spread fanwise all round the manger, their large wondering eyes gazing at the Babe.

'Prr – prr – prr– rr – r', sang the two cats, happy in the presence of their Creator.

The Babe's little hands moved, and touched the soft fur and downy feathers that were so close to Him. The Maiden smiled, a wondering, sweet mother-smile.

Very softly the Choristers took up the note again.

'He cometh down from Heaven and is made man', they sang. 'Glory to God in the Highest; peace on earth to men of good will. Alleluia.'

You can see what happened after that, for you have seen it for yourselves. Only instead of the two lines of waiting choristers you must see the Choir as it was then, filled with hundreds of boys, from side to side, and end to end, all the singing boys who have ever sung there.

They were all robed in soft radiant light. Each bore a lighted taper. Bishop Grandisson and Bishop Oldham entered the Choir. The rows of choristers fell on their knees, and the two Bishops, one on either side, with hand uplifted and outstretched, walked solemnly past the waiting boys, murmuring the familiar words of Christmas blessing.

The minstrels had gone back to their gallery. There they stood, their instruments ready. As the murmur of the Bishops' voices ceased, they gave forth in perfect accord, a great, triumphant peal of sound that echoed from side to side of the Cathedral and up into the roof. Strings and wind and clashing cymbals and voices joined in that glorious Amen in which everything for a brief hour had breath, praised the Lord.

> *Magnificat anima mea Dominum...*
> *Gloria Patri, et Filio, et Spiritui Sancto:*
> *Sicut erat in principium, et nunc, et semper, et in saecula saeculorum.*

The lights faded as the clock gave forth the hour of one. As you turned you saw the great stable space was gone, only a faint glimmer came from the corner where the familiar representation of Bethlehem had been put up by the Cathedral workers the day before. Only two animals remained. The two sleepy cats had stayed close to the manger where they had pushed in, and curled round now in the hay, their two bodies, one gray and one golden, softly rose and fell as they slept. Their gentle breathing was the only sound. Everything else was wrapped in a great peace, the peace of the Christmas dawn.[86]

Notes

1. Frances Rose-Troup, *Exeter Vignettes* (Manchester, 1942), 38–57; W.G. Hoskins, *Two Thousand Years in Exeter* (Exeter, 1960), 33–4; George Oliver, *The History of the City of Exeter* (Exeter, 1884), 62–71; Tony Lethbridge, *Exeter's Royal Vistitors* (Exeter, 1991), 23–5.
2. John Thurmer, 'Services since the Reformation', in Michael Swanton (ed.), *Exeter Cathedral: A Celebration* (Exeter, 1991), 215
3. Arthur Huxley Thompson, *The Cathedral Church of St Peter in Exeter* (Exeter, 1949), 41–2.
4. Public Record Office, E36/223 cited in Margaret Westcott, 'Katherine Courtenay, Countess of Devon, 1479–1527' in Todd Gray, Margery Rowe and Audrey Erskine (eds), *Tudor and Stuart Devon* (Exeter, 1992), 13–38. I am grateful to Miss Westcott for providing additional information from the account.
5. Somerset Record Office, DD WO 57/11/17, edited in Todd Gray, *Devon Household Accounts, 1627–59* (Devon & Cornwall Record Society, NS 38, 1995), 255.
6. Alexander B. Grosart (ed.), *The Complete Poems of Robert Herrick* (1873), II, 270, III, 55–6.
7. John Taylor, *Christmas in and out or Our Lord and Saviour Christ's Birthday* (1652), 6.
8. Todd Gray (ed.), *Devon Household Accounts, I* (Devon & Cornwall Record Society, 1995), 190–1.
9. *Brice's Weekly Journal*, number 33, Friday, December the 24th, 1725.
10. Alex Helm, *The English Mummers' Play* (Woodbridge, 1980), 7.
11. Andrew Brice, *The Mobiad of Battle of the Voice, an Heroi–Comic Poem* (Exeter, 1770), 90.
12. *Exeter Flying Post*, 23 December 1893.
13. Derwent and Sara Coleridge (eds), *The Poems of Samuel Taylor Coleridge* (1852), 303–305.
14. John Bidlake, *The Year, A Poem* (1813), 218–220.
15. Devon Record Office, 1262M/FE72.
16. James Cossins, *Reminiscences of Exeter Fifty Years Since* (Exeter, 1878), 68–72.
17. D. & S. Lysons, *Magna Britannia, Devon* (1822), cccliv.
18. G.T. 'Christmas Pastimes in Exeter Sixty Years Ago', *The Western Antiquary*, December 1883, 165–6.
19. *The Western Times*, 29 December 1876.
20. *Woolmer's Exeter and Plymouth Gazette*, 31 December 1831.
21. J.E., 'Christmas Customs in Plymouth, fifty years ago', *The Western Antiquary*, December 1882, 152.
22. *Woolmers Exeter and Plymouth Gazette*, 31 December 1831.
23. See John A. Kempe, *The Autobiography of Anna Eliza Bray* (1884).
24. Mrs Bray, *Letters*, ii, 117–118.
25. *Conybeare and Dawson's Memoir and Views of Landslips in the coast of East Devon &c* (1840), 3–4.
26. Devon Record Office, 1262M/E29/73.
27. *Woolmers Exeter and Plymouth Gazette*, 1 January 1842.
28. *Woolmers Exeter and Plymouth Gazette*, 31 December 1842.
29. *The Plymouth and Devonport Weekly*, 31 December 1846.
30. *The Plymouth and Devonport Weekly*, 30 December 1847.
31. Devon Record Office, Z19/36/16a
32. Devon Record Office, 1052M/Z2, recipes given at end of book entitled 'Miscelleneous Exercises in Fractions by John Grendon', mid nineteenth century.
33. F. Stockdale, *The Illustrated London News*, Christmas Supplement, 1850, page 500.
34. *Exeter Flying Post*, 30 December 1852; *Woolmer's Exeter and Plymouth Gazette*, 1 January 1853.
35. 'Christmas Morning in Exeter Cathedral', *The Illustrated London News*, December 25 1852.
36. *The Illustrated London News*, 28 December 1854.
37. *Poems by Edward Capern, rural postman of Bideford, Devon* (1856), 83–4.
38. Edmund Gosse, *Father and Son* (1970), 83–4.
39. Sabine Baring-Gould, *Further Reminiscences, 1864–1894* (1925), 109–110.
40. *The Western Times*, 29 December 1865.
41. *The Tiverton Times*, 2 January 1866.
42. *The Western Times*, 29 Dec 1865.
43. *Exeter Flying Post*, 27 December 1865.
44. *The Western Times*, 25 Dec 1866.
45. *Exeter Flying Post*, 27 December 1865.
46. *The Western Times*, 29 Dec 1865.
47. *The Western Times*, 28 December 1866.
48. *The Western Times*, 28 December 1866.
49. Charles Kingsley, *His Letters and Memories of his Life* (1921), 287.
50. *Bideford Gazette*, 3 January 1928; L.B. Wells, Twenty-first report on Devonshire Folklore, *Transactions of the Devonshire Association* (63, 1931), 133–4.
51. *The Western Times*, 1 January 1875.
52. *The Devon Weekly Times*, December 1875.
53. *The Western Times*, 28 Dec 1875.
54. *The Western Times*, 31 December 1875.
55. *The Western Times*, 29 December 1876.
56. Richard Pearse Chope, 'Some Rural Ways in Bygone Days', *The Devonian Year Book* (1923), 56–7.
57. P.F.S. Amery, 'Burning the Ashen Faggot', *Transactions of the Devonshire Association* (11, 1879), 107–108.
58. P.F.S.A., 'Burning the Ashen Faggot', *The Western Antiquary*, December 1881, 143–4.
59. *The Western Morning News*, 17 December 1879.
60. *The Western Morning News*, 17 December 1879.

[61] William Crossing, 'Devonshire Christmas-tide Customs', *The Western Antiquary*, December 1881, 143.
[62] *The Western Times*, 1 January 1884.
[63] *The Western Morning News*, 26 December 1883.
[64] *The Western Morning News*, 26 December 1883.
[65] *Devon and Exeter Gazette*, 30 December 1887.
[66] *The Tavistock Gazette*, 28 December 1888.
[67] *The Western Daily Mercury*, 26 December 1889.
[68] *The Western Daily Mercury*, 26 December 1889.
[69] *The Western Daily Mercury*, 26 December 1889.
[70] *The Western Times*, 2 January 1891.
[71] *The Western Times*, 1 January 1892.
[72] *The Western Daily Mercury*, 27 December 1892.
[73] *The Western Times*, 27 December 1895.
[74] *The Devon Weekly Times*, 24 December 1895.
[75] *Exeter Flying Post*, 24 December 1897, editorial.
[76] *Exeter Flying Post*, 24 December 1897, editorial.
[77] *Exeter Flying Post*, 24 December 1897.
[78] *The Hartland Chronicle*, December 1898.
[79] *The Hartland Chronicle*, January 1901.
[80] *The Western Weekly News*, 26 December 1903.
[81] *The Western Morning News*, 26 December 1911.
[82] *Exeter Flying Post*, December 1913.
[83] *The Teignmouth Post and General Advertiser*, 4 December 1914.
[84] *The Western Times*, 28 December 1923.
[85] R. Pearse Chope, 'Some Rural Ways in Bygone Days', *The Devonian Year Book* (1923), 53–6.
[86] Typescript, Exeter Cathedral Library. The author also wrote *Wisdom Builds a City*.

Sources of illustrations

Pages i, iii, iv, 6-8, Joseph Strutt, *Sports and Pastimes of the People of England* (1801); vii, Devon Record Office, 4577M/Z3 & 3769A/Z5; viii, DRO, 5128M/F21; ix, top, DRO, 1659M/ZE(82) & 5277M/F1/17; x-xiv, xvi, DRO, 1262/E29/73; DRO, xii, top, 4577/M/Z3; xv, bottom left, DRO, 2065Madd/F304, top, 5938Z/Z4; 9-12, *Roxburghe Ballads* (18?); 17, 40, William Stukeley, *Itinerarium Curiosum* (1776); 24, Derwent & Sara Coleridge (eds), *The Poems of Samuel Taylor Coleridge* (1852); 28-9, Westcountry Studies Library, SC1004; 51-2, 101, *Western Weekly News*, 26/12/1908; 88-9, WSL, SC952; 90-1, 96-8, private collection; 106-7, 110, *Devon & Exeter Gazette*, 5/12/1925; 111, *The Western Times*, 10/12/1937. The remaining cards are from DRO, 1262/E29/73 and images from *The Illustrated London News*.